Intelligent Logistics Concepts

Intelligent Logistics Concepts

Improving your supply chain with collaboration and ICT

Edited by

Thierry Verduijn
and Babiche van de Loo

Eburon
2003

ISBN 90 5166 973 9

Eburon Publishers
P.O. Box 2867
2601 CW Delft
The Netherlands
tel.: +31(0)15-2131484 / fax: +31(0)15-2146888
info@eburon.nl / www.eburon.nl

Contents

Preface VII
    A.G.J.M. Hammer (Connekt)

Preface IX
    P. van Hal (KLICT)

1   Intelligent Logistics Concepts:
    Improving Your Supply Chain with Collaboration and ICT 1
    T.M. Verduijn, B.P.A.M. van de Loo

2   Layer Model:
    Levels of Co-operation in Logistics Chains and Networks 9
    P. de Wit

3   Organising Planning and Control of ILC:
    Centralised or Decentralised 25
    B.P.A.M. van de Loo, W. Ploos van Amstel

4   Hub to Higher Performance?
    An Internet Hub for the Vos Logistics Supply Chain 45
    J. van Hillegersberg, J.C.M. Tseng, R.A. Zuidwijk,
    M. van Oosterhout, J.A.E.E. van Nunen

5   Collaborative Planning Round a Fresh Fruit Terminal 77
    G.W. Guis

6   Distributed Rotation Planning for Container Barges
    in the Port of Rotterdam 101
    M. Melis, I. Miller, M. Kentrop, B. van Eck, M. Leenaarts,
    M.C. Schut, J. Treur

7   Travail, Transparency and Trust:
     A Case Study of Computer-Supported Collaborative
     Supply Chain Planning in High-Tech Electronics 117
     H. Akkermans, P. Bogerd, J. van Doremalen

8   ILC SCAN: Lessons from ILC Business Cases 137
     T.M. Verduijn, M. Rustenburg, F.-P. Scheer

Appendices 159

Preface

André Hammer (Connekt)

Connekt is proud to present this book containing the results of the 'Intelligent Logistics Concepts' (ILC), a book that points to important future developments and areas of research. It is part of the knowledge dissemination feature embedded in our 'Mobility Management Programme for Goods Transport'.

Connekt is the innovation network for traffic and transport, set up with a view to incentivising the development of knowledge in the field of mobility and accessibility in the Netherlands. In the management of this process, Connekt plays a key role within the dynamics of government, the business community and knowledge institutions. In the 'Programme Mobility & Freight', Connekt contributes toward the comprehensive design of innovative and intelligent distribution networks for both urban and domestic logistical chains. Connekt is currently working on a family of new distribution concepts, which includes Distrivaart, Citybox and Underground Logistics System Tilburg. The aim of this concept family is to help enhance liveability in the Netherlands and reinforce its competitive position.

It has become apparent that factors such as information and communication technology (ICT), transhipment technology and the standardisation of loading units play a crucial part in the development of new distribution networks. Collaborations that transcend the business level – not only between private parties but also with government agencies – is a point at which concepts often tend to fail. These aspects have been given additional attention in our 'Programme Mobility & Freight', be it in the comprehensive design of new concepts such as Distrivaart, or, where necessary, in research activities in which these critical factors are the key element.

Information and communication technology (ICT) support is essential for the logistic control of networks in which several organisations participate. Developments in this field are taking place at such speed that we have set aside a special part of this programme entitled 'Intelligent Logistics Concepts' to cover this aspect. The aim of this programme section is to use ICT to bring businesses in the logistics network into line with one another, enabling them to exchange data, enhance transparency and improve their planning. Optimum planning involves deploying the means as efficiency as possible to ensure that goods arrive at the correct destination in a reliable manner. This is perfectly in line with Connekt's motto 'Reliable Accessibility'.

In the meantime, the entire knowledge cycle has been completed. Having defined knowledge issues and established the state of the art, we have set up certain business cases in business chains and networks so that we can determine the potential of Intelligent Logistics Concepts. Pilots have been implemented in those chains that have high potential. Vos Logistics and Flora Holland (formerly flower auction Holland) are a case in point. The key aspect of these examples is the Logistics Datahub, a central, independent data exchange method.

The information acquired in these projects has been disseminated via newsletters, workshops, the ILC conference in November 2002 and in reports available on request from Connekt. This book provides an overview of the research results and the developments during the past four years of 'Intelligent Logistics Concepts', as well as a vista into important research fields and future developments, such as Intelligent Agent Technology.

I wish you interesting reading!

André G.J.M. Hammer
General Manager of Connekt

Preface

Paul van Hal (KLICT)

The network economy in which players with differing roles work together closely to establish an optimum value chain – is an auspicious development that not only offers economic growth potential but may also solve spatial economic problems. This is the aim KLICT is looking to achieve.

The letters KLICT are an acronym for the Dutch words for *chain networks, clusters* and *ICT*. KLICT aims to gather both generic and directly applicable knowledge in the field of chain and network science and subsequently make it available to businesses and public organisations. This includes knowledge of the structure of chains, the dynamics of the transactions in the chain, the problems encountered in the creation of chains and the subsequent management of chains and networks. This knowledge makes it possible to find ways of allowing chains to function more efficiently and effectively and thus generate higher productivity across the board. The chain is typically a structure at meso level, while higher productivity generates results that are measurable at macro level. Increased speed and lower transaction costs mean that higher profits can be made at a lower cost, which in turn enhances one's competitive position. If demand is controlled, there is more perspective to be gained for what is really needed and unnecessary production is therefore avoided. Moreover, available means (and that includes publicly available means) are used more efficiently, thus causing less inconvenience.

During the initial period from 1999 to 2001, KLICT worked on the following nine topics: collaboration in chains and networks, optimising chains, demand chain management, physical innovation of chains, education and knowledge transfer, chains and ICT, social embedding, mainports, and compact valleys. This provided an excellent starting point for initiating a large range of pilot projects. From 2002 onwards, KLICT has been concentrating on the following three core areas, each of which focuses on a clearly defined aspect of chain and network science: demand management capabilities in chains and networks, transparency in chains and networks, and reconfiguration of chains and networks. Demand management capabilities concentrate on the question 'what is needed at the end of the chain?' This leads to a reversal of the chain, in the sense that the question posed at the end of the chain then becomes the starting point for the preceding links in that chain. The second focus field, transparency in chains and networks, contributes to this by indicating how best to pass on the required information in the chain. Finally, this can result in a change, i.e. a reconfiguration in the chain, the third focus field.

Although the above description of the field suggests that it takes the form of a chain, it is important to understand that the field consists, in essence, of networks. The reason for this is that for every organisation that acts as a link in the chain there are more to be found, i.e. colleague firms and competitors, that can have the same connections in the chain. On the other hand, each link has various value flows. The first of these is a physical value flow through which, for example, goods are fed. Secondly, there are information and socio-economical flows that are not running as parallel as they used to and can now follow other organisational paths. This, in turn, reinforces the network aspect.

The same applies to 'Intelligent Logistics Concepts'. An intelligent logistics concept can be seen as a network built up of various elements: a network of physical value flows, the connectivity for electronic data exchange (the information value flow), transparency as to the element pointing towards the importance of trust and collaboration (socio-economic flow), and the planning element in which control and reconfiguration methods are reflected within the network. Dividing the concept into a number of elements makes it possible to employ various disciplines for describing and studying the individual flows. The added value of chain and network science is that these value flows – and in particular their interactivity – can be integrated with one another.

Case research is the core method used by KLICT to gather knowledge. This may take the form of pilots and Multi Client Studies (MCS) involving both the business community within a specific chain and knowledge institutions. Moreover, extra attention is given to making the results of these pilot projects accessible. For example, each project is clearly defined and described on the web site (www.klict.org). This private-public partnership is an essential starting point for KLICT and acts as a guarantee for the development of knowledge that the business community can use to address social problems.

The results of 'Intelligent Logistics Concepts' are not only presented on the Internet but are also published in a book. The objective of this book is to give a large group of interested people the opportunity to learn about the result. Hence, it fits in well with the ICES/KIS objective of granting the Dutch business community access to the knowledge and the insights gained.

Paul van Hal
Managing director of KLICT

1.

Intelligent Logistics Concepts:
Improving Your Supply Chain with Collaboration and ICT

Thierry Verduijn (Connekt/TNO Inro)
Babiche van de Loo (KLICT/Erasmus Universiteit Rotterdam)

1. The concept

Since the 1990s, two trends have been clearly discernible: the rise of supply chain management and the lightning-speed development of information and communications technology (ICT). Growing competition in both national and international markets forces companies as well as entire supply chains to respond effectively to the changing requirements of customers and to optimise the efficiency of the production and service provision processes. There is an increasing awareness that individual companies are less and less able to meet these requirements on their own and that collaboration within the supply chain is necessary. Christopher (1992) has explained that there is competition not only between companies but also within the supply chain as a whole. ICT makes it possible to collect, process and distribute ever growing amounts of information more and more rapidly. For many years, ICT has been used to control and monitor logistics activities within organisations. Now, transcending company boundaries is necessary and enabled by new concepts that are capable of co-ordinating and optimising the planning and execution of the logistics processes of a number of different organisations. This book refers to these concepts as Intelligent Logistics Concepts.

Intelligent Logistics Concepts (ILC) is founded on three important cornerstones: connectivity, transparency and planning. The first component of practical importance is connectivity. Connectivity means enabling the electronic exchange of information contained in the information systems of various companies. The second component refers to the actual exchange and provision of information. In many cases, the exchange between parties within the supply chain is limited to transaction data (orders). However, in order to best respond to future developments, information on inventories, forecasts and schedules will be essential. The essence of ILC lies in planning and co-ordinating processes using this information. An understanding of the current state of affairs in the supply chain and any future developments enables individual organisations to plan more effectively. In addition, it allows groups of organisations to take joint decisions affecting several links in the chain. However, the willingness to share information without reservations and take joint decisions requires absolute mutual trust.

ILC offers great potential to improve business processes. Streamlining the various processes may result in a reduction of lead times, better utilisation of resources, less communication and administrative activities, improvement of service levels and service reliability, and improved control and management of processes (Barrat & Oliveira, 2001). These improve-ments are just a part of a list of potential benefits that can be realised through better co-ordination of logistics processes and activities. Other significant benefits may arise from long-term supply chain collaboration. Companies might note that a change in supply chain structure, a relocation of physical facilities (warehouses and factories), development of new services that require a high level of co-ordination or another division of tasks along the chain might lead to even greater benefits. Frohlich and Westbrook (2001) recently conducted a study involving 322 companies in the US metal and machine industry, which demonstrated that 'outward facing' organisations that collaborate with clients and suppliers perform much better than 'inward facing', non-collaborating organisations.

It is therefore worthwhile for each company to consider its options for collaboration with suppliers, customers or even rivals to co-ordinate processes more closely and improve its own performance and that of the overall supply chain. The main questions to be answered by organisations are how and when should collaboration take place. According to Barrat (2000) the opportunities for supply chain collaboration may involve different parts of the supply chain. Barrat identifies four main areas for collaboration:

–   *Collaborative demand planning and replenishment*: Supply chain partners work together to assess consumer demand and to determine the most appropriate supply management and replenishment approach to meet this consumer demand.

–   *Synchronised production scheduling*: Buyers and 1st and 2nd tier suppliers work together to harmonise the production of end products and components in such a way as to minimise the finished product and semimanufacture stocks within the supply chain.

–   *Collaborative product development*: The development of products that can be produced or configured in an efficient manner. Examples include modular product designs that allow postponing the assembly of end products.

–   *Collaborative logistics planning:* Co-ordinating physical activities, such as transport and warehousing, between the various parties involved, including transshippers, logistics service providers, carriers and recipients.

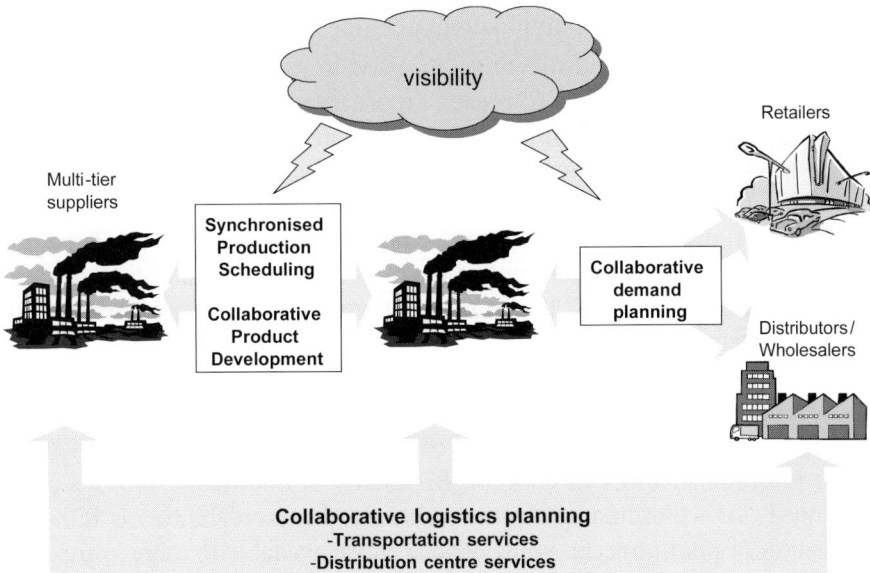

Figure 1: Areas for collaboration in the supply chain (Barrat, 2000)

2. Approach to knowledge development

Although the opportunities and benefits are promising, selecting the right form of co-ordination and achieving effective collaboration with supply chain partners is not a simple task. Despite the fact that numerous concepts for logistics planning and forms of collaboration are known, situational factors and circumstances are important determinants for the success of collaboration. In addition, the manner in which collaboration is brought about impacts the degree of success. In order to determine as comprehensively as possible what form of co-ordination and collaboration is best for each different situation, it is essential that organisations and supply chains learn from one another and share experiences as to what works and what does not.

In the United States, the Voluntary Committee in Inter-industry Standards (VICS) has taken the initiative to co-ordinate the development of the concept of collaborative planning, forecasting & replenishment (CPFR).The mission of this committee is to create collaborative relationships between buyers and sellers through co-managed processes and shared information. By integrating demand and supply-side processes, CPFR will improve efficiencies, increase sales, reduce fixed assets and working capital, and reduce inventory for the entire supply chain while satisfying consumer needs. The VICS stimulates the development of CPFR by bringing manufacturers, retailers, ICT providers and consultants together. Case studies, white papers and meetings are used to exchange methods, results, knowledge and experiences. At present, more than 100 large, internationally-oriented enterprises are participating in this platform.

The ILC innovation programme is comparable to VICS. An initiative of Connekt and KLICT in collaboration with the Holland International Distribution Council (HIDC) and the Royal Netherlands Transport Association, the programme centres on project-based collaboration between companies, both shippers and logistics service providers, government and knowledge institutes for the purpose of developing, applying and disseminating knowledge relating to ILC. In order to devise the most realistic concepts possible, development processes have been created – and still are being created – by and in collaboration with the industry, using pilots to establish proof of concept. By means of knowledge projects about the need for co-ordination within chains, the availability of ICT and evaluation of pilot projects, knowledge is made available to other companies that did not participate in the projects.

This book was written to make the insights gained within the innovation programme in the period 2000-2002 accessible to a broader public. It contains a mixture of practically-oriented approaches to ILC and more theoretically-oriented contributions. The book focuses on collaborative demand planning and replenishment and collaborative logistics planning. Section 3 provides a brief overview of the content of the book.

3. Content and structure of the book

This book elaborates the various aspects of ILC. The issues of connectivity, transparency, business planning and building trust and relationships for collaboration are highlighted using a number of projects that have been carried out over the last three years as part of and outside of the programme. Of course, the discussion of the issues related to collaborative planning in supply chains is not exhaustive nor can we discuss the results of the various projects in detail. However, we hope that we have selected an interesting combination of papers that provide more insight in the opportunities of combining information technology and supply chain management.

– *Overview of business networks.* To explain the role and position of ILC in supply chains, Pieter de Wit presents a view on business networks and the need for close collaboration. The view consists of a three-layered model of business networks. Information technology and more specifically collaborative planning are essential in connecting these business layers and co-ordinating the various processes and actors. The challenges of developing and implementing ILC, some of which will also be further elaborated in this book, are introduced by de Wit.

– *Organising for co-ordination.* Babiche van de Loo and Walther Ploos van Amstel outline considerations that play a role in organising and integrating ILC into supply chains. The key question is which link in the supply chain is the most suitable for decision-making. On the one hand, the availability of additional, more reliable information enables centralisation of chain control. On the other, there are still autonomous organisations that wish to retain control of their business operations. A decentralised approach ensures faster responses to changing circumstances, and the general effects of local decisions and overall progress of processes can be adjusted relatively quickly at the central co-ordination level. The authors draw a parallel with central and local logistics decision-making within organisations and extend the analogy to logistics decision-making in ILC.

– *Connectivity.* A precondition for effective planning is interconnecting the information systems. This is especially important in sectors involving an intensive exchange of information between parties. An example of such a sector is the container industry. In Chapter 3, Van Hillegersberg et al. explain the concept of the logistics data hub. The data hub is used as an information/communication platform for the exchange of data between railways, inland navigation, road transport and terminals. This system does away with the many bilateral contacts and enables each chain party to communicate with the data hub, which takes care of the further distribution of the information. Van Hillegersberg et al. discuss the impact of the data hub on transport chain performance and position the logistics data hub to serve other platforms and concepts.

– *Transparency.* When different parties in the chain provide each other with information, each of these organisations will be able to draw up a more accurate logistics schedule. An early transfer of information reduces uncertainty within the chain, potentially offering various planning benefits. In Chapter 4, Egbert Guis discusses the manner in which the Fruitful project succeeded to increase the transparency of a supply chain of South African fruit to the Netherlands. In spite of the logistics benefits of full transparency in the chain, commercial reasons prevent parties from being fully open about which shipments are underway.

- *Planning.* The project that Marco Melis, Ian Miller and Michael Kentrop describe in Chapter 6 is an elaboration of a decentralised planning approach based on a new technology. It involves improved planning of terminal calls by container inland navigation ships at various container terminals in Rotterdam. The productivity of inland navigation can be improved if the servicing times of the ships at the various terminals are minimised and the reliability of planning can be enhanced. There are often changes and delays during servicing that require the process to be planned all over again. In order to optimise the information exchange between and decision-making by these parties, the planning system is developed using agent technology.

- *Collaboration.* ILC is based on collaboration within chains and networks. Companies are usually not prepared to release information about their own processes and make themselves dependent on others until they feel that they can trust the other party. To ensure this trust, companies will have to consult intensively with one another about the how and where of ILC. Chapter 7 describes how two suppply chain partners went about setting up chain collaboration. It is based on Travail, which indicates that collaborative planning is a process that requires concerted efforts in order to be successful. Henk Akkermans, Paul Bogerd and Jan van Doremalen describe how the collaboration between a supplier of integrated circuits and a major client materialised.

- *Selection of the type of chain co-ordination.* The need and possibilities for logistics co-ordination in chains may differ significantly from situation to situation. Differences in the nature of the process, the importance of information and the type of product lead to a different need for co-ordination. Despite the existence of a number of more or less standard business models for Vendor Managed Inventory (VMI) and CPFR, the chain parties will often have to find out for themselves which form of co-ordination offers the most benefit and is the most appropriate for their respective situations. Chapter 8 uses the lessons from ILC business cases to outline the contours of a method of identifying the possibilities of ILC.

Finally, in the appendices, Connekt and KLICT provide an overview of the various projects that have been carried out within the ILC programme.

4. References

Barrat, M. (2000), *The rise of collaboration in the supply chain,* course material, Cranfield University, Cranfield.

Barrat, M./Oleivera, A. (2001), "Exploring the experiences of collaborative planning initiatives", International Journal of Physical Distribution and Logistics Management, Vol. 31, No. 4, pp. 266-289.

Christopher, M. (1992), *Logistics and Supply Chain Management,* Financial Times Pitman Publishing, London.

Frohlich, M.T./Westbrook, R. (2001), "Arcs of Integration", Journal of Operations Management, Vol. 19, pp. 185-200.

TNO Inro (2002), *Intelligente Logistieke Concepten: Kennis en Strategie fase 1* (Intelligent Logistics Concepts: Knowledge and Strategy Phase 1), TNO Inro report, Delft.

www.cpfr.org.

2.
Layer Model: Levels of Co-operation in Logistics Chains and Networks

Pieter de Wit (HIDC)

Abstract

As a result of market and technological developments, international shippers are drawing heavily on logistics in order to meet the many individual requirements customers have. The extent to which shippers manage the production, storage and transport network and their ability to deal competitively and flexibly with customer orders determines the success of companies in responding to the opportunities offered by the expanding market. This chapter describes the complexity of managing business networks and how new ICT-based logistics concepts can be used to support companies in dealing with this complexity. Shippers and transporters are well aware of the possibilities that information technology offers for improvement of the logistics chain. With regard to inter-company exchange of information, emphasis still lies on orders and transactions, with little attention being given to the exchange of planning data.

1. Introduction

Rapid economic and technological developments are making the logistics terrain more diverse and complex. Many have already concluded that future developments will be difficult to predict. One possible scenario is that the Netherlands could develop into a hub in a global network. A hub where knowledge, information, goods and trade flows may be exchanged, possibly resulting in value-enhancing activities.

One thing is certain, those who can offer better solutions in the area of information in logistics chains and/or processes in the near future can also strengthen their competitive position and possibly extend it. The Netherlands will have to aim for such a development and take a position in the dynamic field of influence. Firmly committed to knowledge development, innovative ability and knowledge-sharing in the logistics sector, the Holland International Distribution Council (HIDC) feels it must make a contribution to this development.

In 2000, the Intelligent Logistics Concepts (ILC) programme was launched in co-operation with various partners. The aim of the programme is to develop an outlook in the area of logistics management, planning and chain or network creation in relation to new ICT applications.

2. Increasing complexity makes heavier demands on logistics

As a result of developments in the market and technological innovations, logistics and distribution are becoming increasingly complex in nature (NDL, 1998).

a. Market developments: individualisation, globalisation, and outsourcing of logistics

Consumers' increasing individualisation is creating a demand for more specialised products and tailor-made services (mass individualisation). More-over, these products and services are required at increasingly short notice – time-to-market periods of 24 hours or less (flexibilisation) are becoming more and more common. Due to such developments as the rise of the Internet, possibilities are being created for direct world-wide interaction between suppliers and customers (globalisation). As a result of growing international competition, more and more companies are focusing on their core activities and contracting out their logistics activities (outsourcing).

b. Technological developments: ICT and logistics software applications

Due to progressive technological developments, companies find it more attractive to outsource logistics activities. A link between the shippers' ERP and/or CRM system and the logistics service providers' TMS and/or WMS systems enables shippers to meet the increasing demands of customers. During logistics performance, deviations from the planning can be reported swiftly via GPS, sensors and tracking and tracing applications, so that prompt corrective action can be taken. In addition to these technological developments on the supply side, there are also various developments on the demand side, of which e-business applications and mobile communication are two of the most important.

The electronic exchange of information in logistics chains and the fact that this leads to improvements in the logistics chain as a whole is nothing new, of course. Many companies already have a type of electronic message exchange with their suppliers, buyers or logistics partners. The innovation is mainly to be found in applications that extend beyond the individual company, viz. emphatic co-operation with partners in the chain. Via e-marketplaces, data hubs, communities and agents, companies can gather information from the chain in a verifiable and safe manner in order to jointly arrive at a better harmonisation of multiple logistics activities in the entire chain.

The exchange of planning data and data on available capacity enables partners to anticipate. This transparency not only increases the insight of every chain party into the activities of the logistics chain, it also facilitates the development of new concepts and planning tools focused on the efficient organisation of chain processes (optimisation) and on the design of the most effective logistics network.

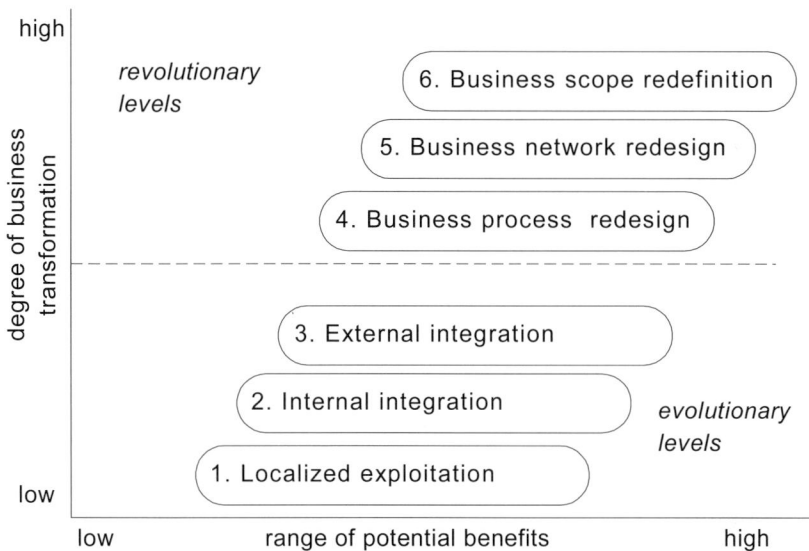

Figure 1: Development stages of ICT applications (source: Venkatraman, 1991)

These new ICT applications have an enormous impact on the logistics chain. According to analogies by Venkatraman (1991), six levels can be distinguished for the impact of ICT (see figure). The lower two levels concern the use of ICT for the support of a number of company functions such as production (level 1) and the integration of existing functions within an organisation (level 2). Supplementary to Venkatraman, an external integration of processes can also be distinguished, where harmonisation of chain partners' processes takes place at performance level. This relates to the purely electronic exchange of existing information, with a more direct link being created between internal and external processes. None of the three primary levels require a change in the working method. The fourth level consists of business process redesign within an organisation. By improving the quality of the information, internal processes are arranged and controlled differently at this level. At the fifth level, processes from outside the organisation are included in the design of the production chain for a product or service. Finally, at level six, the organisation proceeds to redefine its own activities as a result of possibilities and opportunities created by ICT.

In terms of the development stages of applications, many companies are located at levels 3 and 4 and are therefore on the brink of radical changes. These ICT-supporting tools enable companies to plan logistics processes more effectively. New logistics concepts facilitate the improvement of logistics process management, as a result of which the entire logistics chain can be redesigned or improved.

- *New links in the chain - infomediaries:* companies transforming the improvement and processing of information into a core activity. This entails the ability to work with information, rather than just possessing information and infrastructure. The core of their added value consists of making logistics chains more transparent and using this as a basis for supplying services that enhance efficiency and effectiveness.

- *New working methods and forms of co-operation:* In order to make and keep ICT applications operational, it is essential that the various links in the chain work together closely and exchange information intensively. Trust plays a very important role in this respect. It is important to keep looking beyond one's own company, as well as looking ahead and behind in the logistics chain. A link should not be focused on optimising its own effectiveness and efficiency in the logistics chain, but should be concentrating on all company and supra-company activities that may influence the working of the supply chain.

As a result of market and technological developments, international shippers are drawing heavily on logistics in order to meet the many individual requirements customers have. The extent to which shippers manage the production, storage and transport network and their ability to deal competitively and flexibly with customer orders determines the success of companies in responding to the opportunities offered by the expanding market.

3. The layer model

In order to manage the complexity outlined in the previous chapter, it is first of all necessary to gain a better understanding of the logistics network of activities, from the receipt of a customer's order to the delivery and use of the product by that customer. The term logistics network rather than logistics chain is being used deliberately, because more and more products are being processed and handled via a network of parties instead of via a linear chain of parties. In our opinion, a logistics network consists of three levels: (1) the business level, (2) the level of information exchange between the parties and (3) the logistics performance level.

The classification in three levels is based on the process of receipt of customer orders (the business between consumers and shippers at level 1), the actual performance of these orders in the logistics network (level 3) and the necessary facilitating information flows (level 2). Initiatives in the market can be observed in which this classification can be recognised, e.g. in the telecom, automotive, fast-moving consumer goods en high-tech industries. Large international companies (the business owners) such as Nokia, Cisco Systems, IBM, Unilever and Benetton are increasingly outsourcing their product realisation processes to specialised suppliers of production and logistics services (the orchestrators). These activities are controlled and managed by means of world-wide information exchange between supplier and commissioning party. The business owners can then concentrate on the most effective and efficient performance of their core activities.

3.1. The business owner level: more and more orchestrators are being hired

In order to strengthen their international competitive position, international companies with strong brand names will increasingly focus on management of their brands and the relationship with customers. Marketing, product development and strategic purchasing are the business owners' most important in-house activities. Increasingly, external specialists are being hired for supporting processes. Specialised call centres maintain contacts with customers, production is outsourced to contract manufacturers, and logistics activities are performed by logistics service providers. These suppliers and service providers can be directed by the business owners themselves, but it is also possible to engage an external party for this purpose (a supply chain manager or an orchestrator).

Case study: TNT as orchestrator of Compaq's European logistics spare parts network

In 2000, Compaq Global Supply Operations and TNT Logistics concluded a contract under which TNT acts as orchestrator for Compaq's spare and service parts supply in Europe. In this strategic alliance, TNT Logistics has designed and implemented a new logistics infrastructure for Compaq. This implementation was carried out in approx. 12 months; the five-year contract has a value of EUR 227 million. TNT Logistics is responsible for the receipt of spare and service parts, management of the central stock, European distribution, storage in Rapid Fulfilment Centres (RFCs) and the final supply to the service customer. For this purpose, TNT Logistics has set up a 20,000 m2 central ECD in Nijmegen, the Netherlands. In addition, 90 regional RFCs have been set up in 31 different countries. The aim is to offer all Compaq customers in Europe a 2- to 4-hour service. TNT Logistics has a central information system that provides an overview of stock levels throughout the network. This is the only way in which the Compaq service and spare parts orders can be managed flexibly and responsively. In the future, TNT Logistics will use the Compaq central EDC and the RFCs for other customers as well. This multi-use approach creates synergetic benefits that enable TNT Logistics to work more efficiently while simultaneously offering an improved service to customers (source: TNT Logistics website).

The business owners remain in charge of interaction with the customer, but they are making increasing demands on orchestrators in the logistics network for the performance of the fulfilment process. Partly as a result of the emergence of e-commerce, companies are having to deal with new global distribution channels and increasingly dynamic customer demands, requiring close harmonisation with the logistics network layout. The structure in which retail warehouses are continually supplied from a central warehouse is different than a structure in which orders from individual customers are handled. In order to optimise the capacity of the logistics network, companies are increasingly using process-oriented e-procurement marketplaces, where a large number of potential suppliers are provided with an overview of the demand for products and services. In this way, networks of suppliers and (contract) production locations are emerging alongside the traditional, stable, fixed chains.

3.2. The information exchange level: interlinking and transparency of information flows

This second level in the logistics network consists of the exchange of information flows between the various parties in the network with a view to handling customer orders. Various information systems of suppliers, logistics service providers and the business owner are linked; traditionally, via EDI links, but the Internet is also being used more and more. The open character of the Internet offers a rapid, cheap and transparent presentation of order and transaction information, and the possibility to share this with a large number of parties in the network. This transparency provides opportunities for improvements in planning, management and optimisation of the logistics processes. An example is the use of APS (Advanced Planning and Scheduling) tools to realise chain optimisations. The key to success in such networks lies in the effective sharing of information between various parties in the network, which facilitates planning based on actual information, rather than on forecasts or outdated information.

The use of public and private marketplaces is increasing rapidly, particularly for procurement applications. These marketplaces can be divided into two categories:

1. *Network management marketplaces:* concerns the outsourcing of a package of (logistics) activities by a business owner to an orchestrator. Such outsourcing nearly always relates to long-term business contracts, which are only concluded once every so often. Relatively little use is made of the Internet for this category of marketplace. The contract between business owner Compaq and Orchestrator TNT Logistics is a good example.

2. *Process management marketplaces:* concerns the outsourcing of (logistics) activities by an orchestrator to lower-tier logistics service providers. Here, the emphasis lies on achieving optimal efficiencies in the logistics network by combining purchasing, flows and stocks, etc. Services purchased are often used in the short term, and depend on customer demand. These process management marketplaces are far more Internet-oriented. Logistics performance at transora.com is a good example.

Case study: Transora.com, the global e-marketplace for Consumer Packed Goods

Transora.com is the leading global e-marktplace for the consumer packaged goods industry. Transora was set up in 2000 to support consumer goods multinationals in the redesign and optimisation of their international distribution networks; the keyword is co-operation between companies. Companies such as Cadbury Schweppes, Heineken, Procter & Gamble, Sara Lee and Unilever are at the forefront of the transora.com initiative in Europe. In the US, the Transora community uses Transplace, a leading Internet-oriented provider of transport management services, in order to improve efficiency and save costs by means of co-operation. Transplace is a new company set up by six large American logistics service providers (including J.B. Hunt) and acts as the orchestrator in the transora.com logistics network. The core service of Transplace is the Dense Network Efficiency system, which seeks the best match between the shipper's freight and the transporter's capacity. This avoids wasted miles and long waiting times, while improving the degree of loading (the use of transport) (source: www.transora.com).

3.3. The supply network level: optimal use of resources in logistics performance

At this third level, the physical activities required to handle customer orders are performed. This entails the performance of production, storage and transport processes, and involves suppliers, contract manufacturers and logistics service providers. Production can, for instance, take place at local level according to the principles of producing to order, producing to stock, value added logistics and postponed manufacturing. In this way, the demand for individual projects that have to be supplied within a short period can be met. In the case of storage design within the logistics network, concepts such as central and/or regional distribution centres, storage satellites and storage points in the market are distinguished. Finally, transport can take place by direct supply, merge-in-transit or cross-dock operations for consolidating, sorting and distributing shipments.

Case study: PFSweb as e-fulfilment centre for the Adidas European e-commerce channel

PFSweb is a Benelux-based logistics service provider whose focuses include offering complete e-fulfilment solutions in Europe. One of PSFweb's most important customers is Adidas. Adidas was the first major sportswear company to sell its products directly to customers via the Internet. The development of e-commerce opportunities was an important part of the Adidas e-tail strategy, where contact with retail partners also had to be maintained. The on-line Adidas shop uses the PFSweb e-fulfilment solution, specifically for stock management, order processing, distribution and return logistics. The PFSweb fulfilment system has a direct link to the Adidas website. Customer orders are forwarded directly from the Adidas website to the PFSweb, which then handles the logistics of the order. This is accomplished in the PFSWeb warehouses using RF equipment, pick to light systems, automatic put away and replenishment concepts, as well as transport belts. By using these automatic systems, PFSweb is able to meet the delivery times and reliability requirements agreed with Adidas.

The framework outlined above can be an aid to shippers in trying to understand the complex logistics market and the possibilities of tailor-made logistics solutions. Logistics service providers have long concentrated on the performance of logistics processes in networks, for which they have the necessary means of transport, logistics centres and knowledge of operational processes. However, several large and innovative service providers will be concentrating more and more on orchestrating complex logistics processes for their customers. These service providers, in particular, only issue directions and no longer possess any physical means of transport in other words, they are non-asset based. A condition for fulfilling this orchestrator role is that these service providers integrate the required innovative ICT systems and process management skills seamlessly into their organisation.

4. Growing demand for ICT

It can be concluded from the previous chapter that traditional logistics concepts are susceptible to change as a result of an increased diversity in product categories and service characteristics. It is clear that a single standard solution is no longer sufficient. Closer co-operation in chains or networks offers a solution for anticipating the many and diverse customer demands. In this respect, the development of level 2, the information exchange level, is essential.

If the information exchange level is studied in more detail, the three layer model can be extended into four layers: logistics network, connectivity, transparency, and network design and management. Together they comprise an Intelligent Logistics Concept.

– *Logistics Network:* all companies are part of a logistics network and they all conduct business with other parties in that network. Agreements are made beforehand concerning the service to be provided, information and/or money. These processes are standardised where possible. ERP, TMS and WMS are applied for the management and support of logistics processes in each of the links in the logistics network.

– *Connectivity:* a pre-requisite for ICT applications is that companies are able to exchange data electronically. In addition, it is important that data available in internal systems such as ERP, WMS and TMS, and formats and meanings are clear and unequivocal. Key words are connections, accessibility and routing. Solutions that are important for the realisation of connectivity include: Internet connections, message scenarios, databases and links/interfaces with existing systems.

– *Transparency:* this means that companies share information about the chain so that each company has a better understanding of the logistics chain. For transparency or, to put it differently, data sharing, co-operation and trust are essential: companies must be prepared to share (confidential) information about processes with other partners in the chain.

– *Network design and management:* on the basis of availability of data and an overview of the logistics chain, applications or tools can be developed that support chain partners in the optimisation of the logistics chain. These improvements may relate to a better harmonisation of the various links and processes in the current chain, or a redesign of the existing chain. As a result of the growing demand in logistics chains, the emphasis will lie more and more on tools that search for improvements in the network in real-time.

The ILC structure in four different layers can be compared to the principle of Maslov's pyramid, i.e. connectivity must be realised before transparency and planning tools are considered. Unfortunately, as connectivity cannot yet be taken for granted via the Internet, it still requires the necessary attention.

In practice, each party (or chain) is trying to get to grips with the realisation of the above ICT components. In several exploratory sessions last year, the *need for* and *the application possibilities of ICT* in specific logistics chains were identified. Discussions were held with shippers (business owners, level 1) and transporters/logistics service providers (performers, level 3).

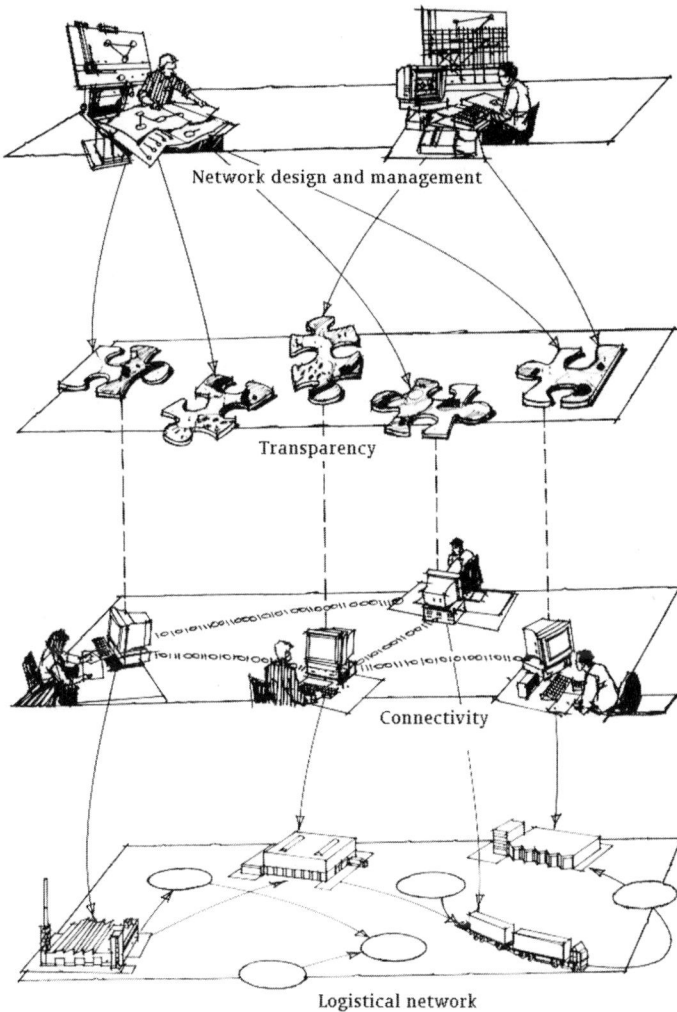

Figure 2: the components of an Intelligent Logistics Concept

Shippers:

ICT need

All shipping parties have radically centralised the management of their own logistics chain, usually with a view to improved control and the creation of economies of scale. As a result of growing service demands, logistics chains are assuming a greater global range, more and more goods flows are effected directly and storage capacity is being eliminated. This has enormous impact; the logistics chain is developing into a logistics network and the number of contact points within this network is expanding drastically. The number of logistics partners has also been reduced to a few strong players. As customer demands, degrees of service, laws and regulations, etc., differ from country to country, the strong logistics partners subcontract local specialists. Shipping partners have concluded that it is not possible for a single logistics service provider to offer an overall pan-European service. Co-ordination is therefore required.

ICT experience

All shipping parties are investing heavily in ICT. However, it appears that companies are investing mostly in their own systems in their own business environment. There is a strong focus on standardisation of ICT systems. System integration with partners and customers is still in its infancy. On the supply side, a tentative start is being made with purchasing clusters (e.g. e-procurement portals) and marketing clusters (e.g. e-marketplaces with product information). On the distribution side, there is still a great deal of e-mail, telephone and fax communication. There is already frequent control and communication with large partners in the chain via EDI. The transparency in the chain is provided by the tracking and tracing services of the large integrators and logistics service providers. Although this yields on-line transparency, there is insufficient anticipation of the available information. In general, too little use is being made of the Application Service Providers (ASP, to encourage chain communication) and Advanced Planning and Scheduling systems (APS, to encourage chain planning).

Transporters/logistics service providers:

ICT need

Transporters are aware of the restrictions of their own distribution network. Consequently, large service providers engage local specialists to supplement their own network. Smaller logistics parties select local partners. The European network of a logistics service provider thus consists of a large number of small companies. Services, expertise and cultures often clash, which obstructs centralised European management and performance. As a result, the utilisation of own networks is also far from ideal.

ICT experience

Service providers use many different ICT systems (ERP, WMS, TMS, legacy system, etc.). System integration often proves difficult due to tailor-made solutions and the many system upgrades. The difficult communication between systems limits the possibilities for chain optimisation. Moreover, the introduction of new services has traditionally been based on the upgrading of old systems. This is an expensive business if you are a service provider and also the only system owner and system developer. Consequently, many service providers are now purchasing standard packages. In the distribution environment, however, standard packages are still proving inadequate when it comes to meeting the demands of service providers. Customers and customers of customers are all demanding a special report format.

Shippers and transporters are well aware of the possibilities that information technology offers for improvement of the logistics chain. However, attention is still focused primarily on internal logistics concepts and solutions: the harmonisation of IT applications and ERP in particular within the own organisation. Co-operation in networks is proving difficult, particularly when a limited number of permanent partners are being sought at a global level. As regards supra-company exchange of information, emphasis still lies on orders and transactions, with little attention being given to the exchange of planning data.

5. Steps towards ILC

In practice, the focus is often on realising connectivity. Co-operation within the chain is so expensive and time-consuming that development processes are slow and protracted. The thorny question is that the various partners in the different layers often do not speak the same language. In addition, shippers are still reluctant to share planning data freely with their logistics partners. Accordingly, the orchestrator role outsourced to a logistics service provider is still a rare phenomenon, and there is still a great deal of virgin territory and much room for improvement.

The question of whether the use of new ICT applications actually leads to a better result is difficult to answer. We assume it does, but every project is, of course, unique! Knowledge gained from the ILC programme provides guidelines for assessing impacts, opportunities and yields. Guidelines relating to:

- *Financial matters:* how much does the new ICT application cost and what does it offer? How can yields be apportioned to the various parties in the chain?

- *Commercial matters:* does the new ICT application lead to extra turnover, new markets and/or changes in relationships within the chain?

- *Changes in the internal organisation:* to what extent does the new ICT application influence the individual chain components? For each component, the analysis can focus on three aspects:
    - Operation: does anything change in the day-to-day operations?
    - Organisation: does anything change in the management of the organisation? Does the organisation have the required personnel?
    - Strategy: are there structural changes to the working method of the chain?

6. References

NDL (1998), "European Logistics, In search of excellence in supply chain solutions", The Hague, draft version.

NDL (2000), *European Logistics Concepts, Positioning European logistics concepts in the changing business environment of transparent supply demand networks*, The Hague.

Sheombar, H.S. (1995), *Understanding Logistics Co-ordination*, Tilburg University dissertation, published by Tusein Nolthenius, 's-Hertogenbosch.

SITS (2000), *Simple Intermodal Tracking & Tracing*, Final Report, commissioned by EU DGVII.

Snijders, M. (2001), "OCE centraliseert distributie service parts" (OCE is centralising the distribution of service parts), Tijdschrift voor Inkoop en Logistiek (Purchase and Logistics magazine), Vol. 17, No. 5, pp. 20-22.

TNO Inro (2000), *Voorstudie Intelligente Logistiek Concepten* (Intelligent Logistics Concepts – a preliminary study), TNO Report: Inro-Logistiek/2000-23, Delft.

TNO Inro, Informore, KPMG (2000), *Logistieke Datahub Nederland: Plan van Aanpak* (The Netherlands as Logistics Datahub: Plan of Approach), Rotterdam.

Venkatraman, N. (1991), "IT induces business reconfiguration", in: Allen, T.J./Scott Morton, M.S. (Eds), *The corporation of the 1990's*, Oxford University Press, New York, pp. 122-158.

Verduijn, T./Wit, P. de (2001), "Intelligente Logistieke Concepten: Concepten, Mogelijk-heden, Implementatie en Ervaringen" (Intelligent Logistics Concepts: Opportunities, Implementation and Experiences). In: Rodenburg, R.H.J./Ruijgrok, C.J. (Eds), *Bij-dragen Vervoerslogistieke Werkdagen 2001*, Corssendonk, pp.12.

3.

Organising Planning and Control of ILC:
Centralised or Decentralised

Babiche van de Loo (Erasmus University Rotterdam)
Walther Ploos van Amstel (TNO Inro)

Abstract

Logistics concepts are becoming increasingly sophisticated. For example, Xerox has developed printers that are connected to the Internet via a modem and, when maintenance or a new toner cartridge is required, can relay this information to a service location without the human intervention. This facilitates rapid handling of maintenance and stock management. However, a precondition for this is that the entire logistics and planning process behind maintenance and stock management support and enable this. The development of intelligent logistics concepts (ILC) is not an isolated process. It requires changes to business processes. Within the context of ILC, in addition to issues regarding the design of the logistics network, there are questions regarding ILC management, the use of information and communication technology (ICT), and the division of tasks and responsibilities. The authors examined the last aspect in particular: Who will take decisions regarding ILC? This chapter addresses this organisational question – centralised or decentralised management? First, the background of ILC will be discussed, followed by an elaboration of the choice between a decentralised and a centralised logistical organisation. These are first addressed from an individual company's perspective and then from an inter-organizational ILC perspective.

1. Improved logistical performance demands collaboration

Effective logistics enhance a company's market position. Changing situational factors create new requirements. Logistics management that does not respond in a timely manner can lead to high logistical costs or result in the client not receiving its products at the time requested. Consequently, the company does not achieve its objectives, commercial or otherwise. For this reason, logistics professionals actively respond to situational changes.

Relevant trends for logistics and supply chain management include:

– Transforming products into services. The secretariat no longer simply buys a photocopier, but uninterrupted document flows. The army no longer buys a tank, but strike power. Families no longer buy a TV, but home entertainment. The traditional flow of goods is only part of this process. Co-ordination of several processes is required.

- Increasing speed of the supply chain. This entails shorter lead times, rapid introduction of new products and the implementation of innovation in new distribution channels (e.g. e-commerce).

- Satisfying individual client needs and achieving ever-higher levels of customer service.

- Reducing the costs of operating capital in the supply chain and achieving true synergy in mergers and take-overs. The merger involving the retailer Laurus demonstrates that this is no easy task.

- Increasing profits through the smart use of supply chain management. The success of such companies as Cisco, Viking Direct, Dell and Wal-Mart can largely be attributed to supply chain management.

- Logistics solutions also face requirements as regards sustainability. Situational impact and quality of life are key criteria for logistics solutions such as city distribution, reverse logistics and modal shift.

The Council of Logistics Management (CLM) frequently commissions studies into the consequences that changing situational factors have for logistics and supply chain management. The '21st Century Logistics' study shows how the focus of logistics has changed in the past decades (CLM, 1999). The focus of logistics first shifted from efficiency and costs to the quality of logistics (i.e. customer service). It then moved to more comprehensive approaches, in which service levels and financial objectives were integrated. Finally, the attention shifted from an internal to an external outlook through partnerships with clients and suppliers, external integration and supply chain management.

CLM (1999) posits that logistical integration should be approached at six levels:

1. *Customer integration* entails the identification of the long-term requirements and preferences of current/potential clients. To offer a client added value, a company must base its efforts and approach on this insight.

2. *Internal integration* demands the integration of all fundamental activities within a company to achieve high external logistical performance at an acceptable internal cost.

3. *Supplier integration* entails the perfect orchestration of the supply of services, raw materials, ancillary materials and semi-manufactures as well as of the exchange of information. Achieving this yields a single integrated process.

4. *Technology and planning integration* entails the development and maintenance of ICT. This enables clients to actually be linked up with suppliers. To the extent that management was involved with the internal flow of goods, it is now also required to handle the co-ordination with clients and suppliers.

5. *Measurement integration* must enable tracking the performance of all parties in the supply chain. Companies must have unequivocal supply chain performance indicators at their disposal to enable an effective response to disparities in the agreed levels of performance of one or more parties.

6. *Relationship integration* must yield a shared vision of clients and suppliers regarding the objectives to be achieved through collaboration. Efforts must focus on providing the highest value for the client.

Integration and co-ordination
Co-ordination in the company (and more frequently across the entire supply chain) must become more and more accurate. The leeway that once existed for waiting times and stock, for instance, has disappeared. Supply chain processes are interdependent. Management should disregard boundaries (see Figure 1).

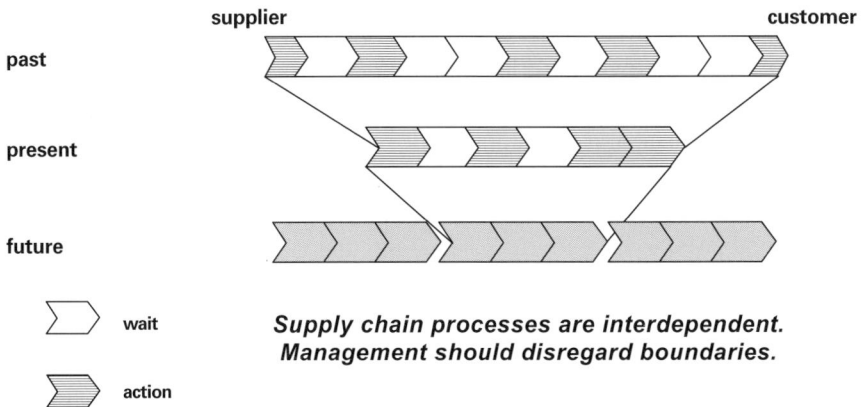

Figure 1: Growing need for co-ordination

Christopher (1998) states 'Companies do not manage this on their own anymore. Competition changes from between companies into between supply chains'. Accordingly, another dimension is added to logistics, more specifically supply chain and network collaboration. Under the motto 'supply chain management', the field of logistics has developed many new concepts to support collaboration and integration (Van Goor et al., 2003). The list is by no means exhaustive, but includes Collaborative Planning, Efficient Consumer Response (ECR), Continuous Replenishment, Vendor Managed Inventory (VMI), Collaborative Planning Forecasting and Replenishment (CPFR), Synchronised Production, Supply Chain Planning, Advanced Planning Systems (APS), Supply Chain Execution software, e-procurement and B2B marketplaces. A relatively new offshoot of logistics, ILC is the focus of this book. ILC often combines several of the supply chain concepts listed above. An example of VMI is presented below.

Case study: Akzo Nobel

A global leader in coatings, Akzo Nobel manufactures paints, enamels and varnishes for the industrial, transport, yacht and shipbuilding, DIY and professional painting sectors. Akzo Nobel also manages the distribution of paints to professional painting companies via wholesalers that are generally owned by Akzo Nobel. The wholesalers maintain stocks of paint and determine delivery schedules and the levels of stock to be maintained. VMI is being considered as a way to centralise this process. To this end, all of the wholesalers have switched to the same ERP system to facilitate the transition to VMI at a later date. VMI enables the centralised management of ordering and production processes at Akzo Nobel. VMI entails a partnership in which the ordering process shifts from the customer to the manufacturer, which then becomes responsible for key financial and customer service indicators. The VMI process is also supported by computer systems and dedicated teams that are designed to maintain a customer's inventory at a predetermined optimal level.

---

2. Intelligent logistics concepts

The rise of advanced ICT, in particular, enables more efficient and effective operations and improved business management. ILC comprise innovative, high-grade concepts that increase supply chain transparency and improve the efficiency and effectiveness of inter-organizational logistics processes. An ILC meets the following criteria:

— *Inter-organizational:* Several parties exchange information. In addition, the parties involved represent at least two consecutive supply chain links.

— *Innovation:* Innovation must play a role. Existing and proven functionalities are introduced in new business environments or new facilities are developed by improving connectivity and logistical co-ordination.

— *ICT component:* The use of ICT plays a decisive role in the co-ordination of inter-organizational logistics. A central element of ILC involves using existing systems to connect to ICT applications in other companies in such a way as to support the required levels of logistics co-ordination.

— *Transparency:* This embodies the actual exchange of information between supply chain partners, which in turn enhances supply chain management.

— *Effectiveness and efficiency:* This means that improved connectivity and digitisation of information flows alone are not enough. Clear improvements in logistical performance must be achieved through changes to the organisation's physical process, based on improved availability of information.

In many ways, ILC is a philosophical approach, which underscores the belief that there remains a great deal of benefit to be gained from the broad field of supply chain co-ordination and planning. In addition, ILC highlights two areas. First, the ILC philosophy clearly outlines the elements required to achieve co-ordination along the entire supply chain, viz. network design, connectivity, transparency (through collaboration), management and planning. The ideal form of management and planning to be employed and the elements to be co-ordinated differ for each situation and supply chain. The previously mentioned supply chain concepts may facilitate decision-making in this regard. Secondly, the philosophy also includes the aspect of supply chain development. After all, the supply chain is not static. Market dynamics will determine whether the composition of the supply chain must be adjusted and whether the supply chain must be reconfigured. These supply chains, too, must be co-ordinated and planned. ILC are designed to improve supply chain efficiency and effectiveness by improving the co-ordination and planning of activities across the entire supply chain. The

Bloemenveiling Holland flower auction is a case in point. Two questions arise: What are the elements of ILC? What is the role of logistical organisation within ILC?

Case study: Bloemenveiling Holland

Each day, Bloemenveiling Holland receives substantial quantities of flowers and plants from growers, destined for a large number of traders and sorted by the auction house using a cross-dock operation. To date, the auction house has only rarely received information from the growers, carriers and traders as to the varieties and quantities shipped and the time at which the flowers and plants will arrive. As a consequence, Bloemenveiling Holland has no information available to plan the unloading of incoming products and the rest of the internal logistics. The carriers are not informed in advance of the quantities they are supposed to collect from the growers, nor of the time at which they can be expected at the auction house. This results in waiting times at the loading and unloading docks.

As part of ILC, a logistical datahub will be installed for the auction house's supply chain. A datahub is an information collection and distribution point. Growers use a datahub to inform the auction house of the quantities they are going to supply and for which dealers the flowers and plants are intended. Using this information, carriers can plan trips to collect the flowers and plants, and Bloemenveiling Holland can plan its internal logistics process and dock-handling. Another possible benefit is co-ordination between the carriers and Bloemenveiling Holland.

The transparency that the logistics datahub offers not only enables each party in the supply chain to improve their own planning, but also allows the various parties involved to co-ordinate their plans.

3. The logistics concept behind ILC

A design model (integrated logistics concept) has been developed for drafting logistics policy (Van Goor, 1992). A characteristic feature of ILC is that decisions regarding (see Figure 2) supply chain strategy, logistics objectives, logistics network and the processes this involves, logistics planning and control, logistical ICT and logistical organisation are taken in a cohesive manner. The manner in which the logistics concept is fleshed out is decisive for logistical performance. For this reason, the concept is supplemented with performance indicators. Constant co-ordination between all of the elements is necessary. The elements of the integrated logistics concepts will be explained later. The concept can also be used in the development of ILC.

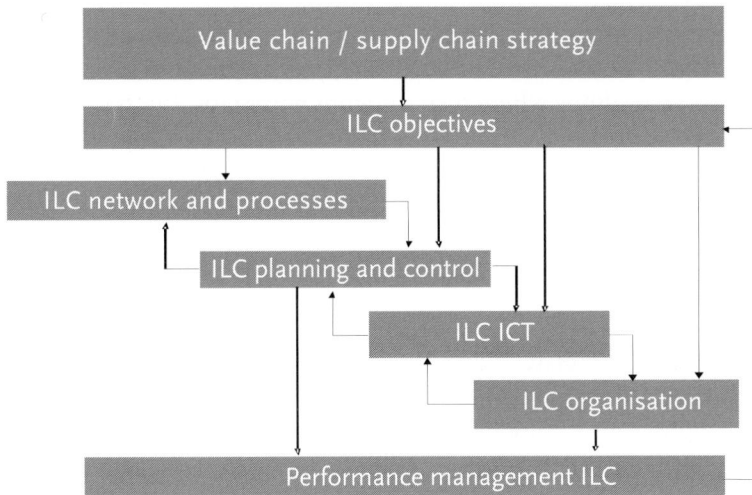

Figure 2: Integrated logistics model (based on Van Goor, 1992)

Supply chain strategy and logistics objectives

Logistics objectives are the result of the competition strategy selected by the companies in the supply chain. Fisher (1997) makes a useful distinction between 'physically efficient' and 'market-responsive' supply chains. Distrivaart, it is a waterway port transport network of pallets operated by a multicompany community platform (for beer breweries and soft drinks company aims to achieve efficient transport of pallets of products with a low value density and, in this sense, is primarily physically efficient. Market responsiveness is achieved through additional road transport. Bloemen-veiling Holland's datahub also aims to achieve improved efficiency. The US Army employs the ILC 'joint total assessment visibility' (JTVA), which has all the characteristics of a 'market-responsive' supply chain (Van Merriënboer et al., 2002). This case study is reviewed below.

Case study: JTVA

The problems encountered during Desert Storm impacted the operational effectiveness of units. Operational units had no overview of the status of their orders. It was unclear whether something had been ordered. In addition, no one knew when and where the goods would be delivered, nor where the goods were in the supply chain. As a consequence, an excessive burden was placed on the logistics system since goods were ordered twice and, consequently, goods were delivered to locations where they were not necessary.

The US Army wants to be able to offer rapid crisis response. One way to achieve this is to give the soldiers better support by increasing responsiveness, transparency and access to logistical resources. The US Army refers to this as 'focused logistics'. JTAV is the term used for the efforts made to gain more insight into the availability of resources. Implementing JTAV enables the US Army to provide users with timely, accurate information regarding the locations, direction of movement, condition and identity of units, personnel, equipment and supplies.

JTAV is implemented in two phases. The first phase entails connecting existing information systems (known as legacy systems) to a central database. All relevant information is stored in this database, which is made available to users via the Internet. The accuracy and currentness of the information depends on the accuracy of the information entered into the database and the frequency with which the information is updated. The second phase involves the transition to a system that extracts information from the existing information systems based on the users' needs. The key difference is that, in the second phase, the information is no longer centrally stored, but retrieved directly from connected information systems via an ICT backbone. This requires intelligent software, which searches for the appropriate information from all the available information systems and makes it available to users requesting the information in a comprehensible language. This intelligent software functions as a 'translator', linking various information systems. The great advantage of the latter approach is that the information supplied is always up to date, provided that the intelligent software accesses information faster than the information is updated.

ILC network and processes

Hoekstra and Romme (1993) describe the logistics foundation as a model that depicts the flow of goods and includes the following elements: primary processes from purchasing to follow-up care, stock locations in the flow of goods and the movement of goods between processes and stock locations. The intermodal network is at the heart of Distrivaart. The manufacturer's pallets are transported to the container ship by road and again from the ship on the way to the retailer's distribution centre. The uncoupling point is on board ship, where anonymous stock can be assigned to concrete orders. At Distrivaart, a great deal of attention goes to the loading and unloading process and to pallet movements on board the barge.

The logistics control model

Once the logistics configuration has been selected, the following question arises: How does the logistics foundation facilitate goods reaching the client in a manner in line with the logistics objectives? Logistics planning and control entails the organisation, planning and management of the flow of goods from the development phase, through to purchasing, production, distribution and, finally, to the end customer in order to achieve the objective of meeting customer needs at low cost and with controlled use of capital. Logistics planning and control has three sub-objectives: satisfy customer needs as much as possible (in terms of delivery times, product specifications, assembly, after-sales service, information provision and flexibility), maximise the use of available capacity in the network of production operations, distribution and transport and after-sales to minimise logistical efforts (costs and operating capital) and allow the most efficient and reliable flow of raw and auxiliary materials, semi-manufactures and end products through the supply chain.

Bertrand (1988) distinguishes three levels of decisions, which offers a solid basis for organising logistics planning and control in ILC:

1. At the strategic/supply chain level

    This entails establishing the basic rules and objectives of logistics policy, including the required capacity load and lead times, level of back-up stock in the network, delivery times and required delivery reliability. It means laying down the preconditions that orders must meet to enable provision of the agreed quality, price and delivery commitments and determines the amount of slack each party has in logistics control.

2. At the tactical/goods flow level

    This is where the future flow of orders for the supply chain parties with
    available capacity in ILC is co-ordinated. Areas addressed include stock
    levels and locations, production planning, determining the capacity of
    the distribution network and drafting a Distrivaart schedule.

3. At the operational/implementation level

    Given the volume of the flow of goods agreed upon at the tactical level
    and the adopted basic rules, operational and implementation
    departments are responsible for the acceptance and fulfilment of the
    work orders generated. This entails the daily scheduling of orders,
    setting priorities for client orders, planning distribution facilities,
    determining the order of transport schedules and proposing delivery
    times to customers.

Logistical ICT

As stated earlier, the use of ICT is a core element of ILC in achieving the
inter-organizational co-ordination of logistics. Logistical ICT supports ILC
processes and their control. Many companies already have integrated ERP
systems and supplementary transport management (TMS) and warehouse
management (WMS) applications. Connectivity represents the ICT
infrastructure required for the electronic exchange of information between
existing systems. ERP systems will continue to be at the heart of registering
functions in particular. This allows seamless integration of all flows of
information within the companies. ERP systems are supplemented with
applications for a wide range of processes (including WMS, TMS, scheduling
software) and APS applications for planning and optimising the supply
chain. The introduction of Business Intelligence Tools completes the ICT
architecture. The Akzo Nobel and Bloemenveiling Holland case studies
discussed earlier demonstrate that ICT is a critical success factor.

Logistical organisation

Logistical organisation addresses the division of roles and responsibilities.
This involves laying down the tasks and responsibilities. In the case of Akzo
Nobel, the operational responsibilities for stock were centralised at the
wholesalers and production management. Co-ordination often gets off to a
slow start. Logistical performance is frequently influenced by decisions made
by employees with different interests. Consequently, constant mutual co-
ordination is required. As stated earlier, as the requirements increase, so

does the need for co-ordination. As a result, some companies decide to centralise logistics management in a single department. Other companies decide to keep logistics management decentralised, leaving the tasks and responsibilities with the functional departments. Organisational structure determines the degree to which the logistical approach of employees bearing responsibility for logistical decisions is integrated (Ploos van Amstel, 2002), as well as the emphases and priorities of their actions. For this reason, logistical organisation is seen as a key factor in achieving effective logistical performance. The case study of Outokumpu is presented as an example of centralised logistics management, particularly at the tactical level.

> Case study: Outokumpu
>
> Based in Kokkola, Finland, Outokumpu is a versatile metals group that operates all over the world. Outokumpu's business focuses include base metals production, stainless steel, copper products and technology. In 2001, Outokumpu signed an agreement to acquire Norzink AS. The Odda-based Norzink plant has an annual zinc production capacity of 150,000 tonnes. It is one of the world's most profitable and cost-efficient zinc producers. Outokumpu acquired Norzink to achieve economies of scale, lower costs and improved use of capacity, as well as a more effective assignment of clients to production locations. This reduced costs of transport, for example. The reduction of costs, assignment of clients to production locations and improved use of capacity is only possible if these locations are managed centrally. An Internet application at the head office in Rotterdam is used to centralise management. The head office determines centrally what needs to be produced, how much and for whom.

4. Achieving integration

In the past, there was little need to co-ordinate supply chain activities. The trends previously identified, however, have given rise to the need for more and more companies to accelerate the speed of the supply chain. Activities must follow one another in immediate succession, take place simultaneously or even be completely integrated. Accordingly, activities must follow each other seamlessly. When working on co-ordination and, to this end, embedding the right co-ordination provisions, it is essential to understand the interrelationships of the activities of the organisation units. Galbraith (1973) believes that the best organisational approach is based on the uncertainty in and diversity of the work. This entails reducing the need for co-ordination by creating slack or establishing autonomous logistical organisation units or improving co-ordination capacity, by investing in integrated ICT or by creating horizontal and lateral relationships by changing the organisational structure.

Slack is created by reducing performance levels. This decreases the amount of information to be processed in performing tasks and prevents the overtaxing of hierarchical channels.

By establishing autonomous logistical organisation units (for instance, product divisions or creating shared service facilities), every organisation unit has the resources, expertise and authority required to make decisions. These departments independently accept orders and implement them within the preconditions agreed upon with regard to load, costs, lead times and quality. From a commercial, economic and technical standpoint, however, the process of creating autonomous organisation units is not endless. In order to achieve effective logistics management, it is not possible to establish overly small product divisions without risk. Accordingly, it is essential to identify other ways of improving co-ordination. Extreme implementation of autonomous organisation units may result in limited advantages of scale, loss of synergistic effects and complete loss of coherence between organisation units.

Investing in integrated ICT facilities may improve co-ordination by enabling more useful information to flow through the organisation. The point of such logistical ICT is, ideally, to achieve a unified online real-time system akin to ERP or APS, Internet applications and agent-based applications.

Supplementing the organisational structure with horizontal and lateral relationships brings decision-making down to a lower organisational level, where the relevant information is available. Galbraith (2000) and De Vries (1999) characterise logistical horizontal and lateral relations as:

1. direct, informal contact between logistics employees who work together to address logistical problems

2. logistics liaisons as links between logistical organisation units that have intensive contact with one another

3. temporary logistics workgroups established to solve logistical problems that involve more than one organisation unit

4. permanent logistics teams that focus on logistical co-ordination problems

5. integrated logistical functions in which the logistical decision-making process is co-ordinated

6. a logistics manager who serves a key or even decisive role in logistics management

Consequently, on the one hand there are both co-ordinating/supportive roles and on the other hand more active/managing roles in which logistics managers themselves determine the logistical decision-making process (See Figure 3). Introducing vertical, horizontal and lateral relationships entails investments, resulting in a heavier burden on the organisation and rising costs. In addition, non-vital but excessive embedded provisions are perceived as disruptive. In many instances, the use of a wide range of co-ordinating provisions may be counterproductive due to an overabundance of rules, procedures, consultation formats and constant territorial disputes among logistics employees. In turn, this can result in supplementary organisational measures that give rise to co-ordination issues. For this reason, a well-considered choice of co-ordination provisions is vital.

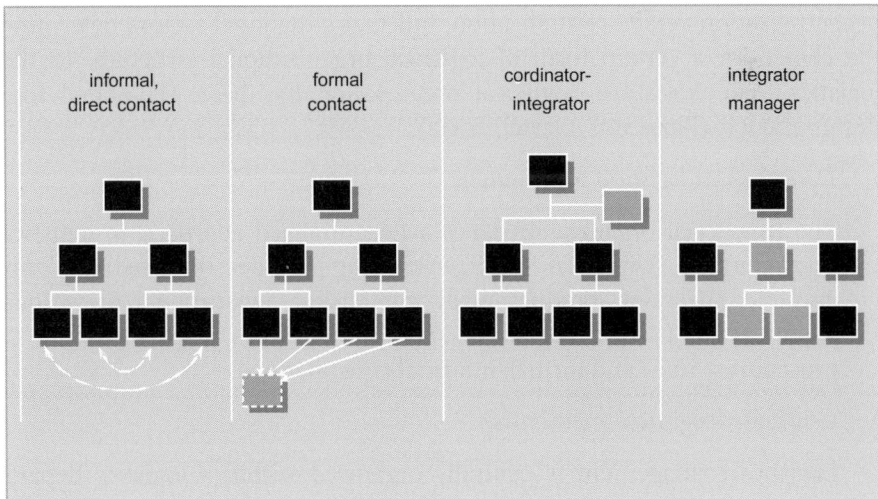

Figure 3: Horizontal and lateral relationships

A recurring question in ILC is whether one wants to centralise or decentralise the supply chain organisation. Centralisation is the strictest method for co-ordinating decision-making (Ploos van Amstel, 2002). A centralised organisation offers certain advantages. Management is transparent, enabling more efficient use of the resource capacity of several parties in the supply chain. This can result in cost savings. Another advantage is that know-how and experience are managed centrally, which benefits several parties.

A decentralised organisation is, of course, another possibility. An advantage is the flexibility to respond quickly to a changing environment. This reduces complexity and employees are empowered to take and bear responsibility for their own decisions. Decisions are made more quickly, enabling the organisation to work more efficiently and effectively. However, this approach lacks having a single person at one centre to oversee all of the consequences of the decisions made. Although decentralisation enables a quick response to changes, a decentralised organisation is less transparent, which makes it difficult to gain an overview of available resources (Mintzberg, 1993), for example. This consideration prompted Outokumpu's decision to centralise its logistics management at the tactical level.

When should one opt for centralised organisation and when for decentralised organisation?

Empirical studies have revealed that this is not merely a matter of decentralisation versus centralisation, but that situational factors determine the choice for a certain form of logistical organisational structure. In the logistics trade literature, logistical organisation has been elaborated into design models (Ploos van Amstel, 2002):

1. *Decentralised logistical organisation*

   The functional organisation takes a decentralised approach to logistics management. Logistical decision-making is decentralised in, for example, the sales, production or purchasing departments or various supply chain parties. Logistical co-ordination takes place according to procedures, rules and formal/informal consultations.

2. *Centralised logistical organisation*

   Logistics management is centrally organised within a logistics department in the form of an integrator manager or co-ordinator manager, who directly manages functional departments and parties by means of purchasing, production or distribution assignment planning. The logistics department is added to the existing functional organisation.

Logistical complexity and predictability determine logistical organisation. When the aim is to reduce complexity and enhance predictability, co-ordination can be realised within the existing structure – decentralised logistical organisation. Tools for this include rules and procedures. If one is confronted with low logistical complexity and logistical predictability, it is necessary to intervene frequently to ensure that the flow of goods remains on track. Co-ordination materialises immediately. A decentralised logistical organisation is characterised by low complexity, offering rapid insight into the consequences of decisions. When logistical complexity is high and logistical predictability low, co-ordination is no longer possible on the basis of the existing hierarchical structure alone. The need then arises for a centralised logistical organisation with an integrator manager. When both logistical complexity and logistical predictability are high, the need for centralised logistical organisation arises (See Figure 4).

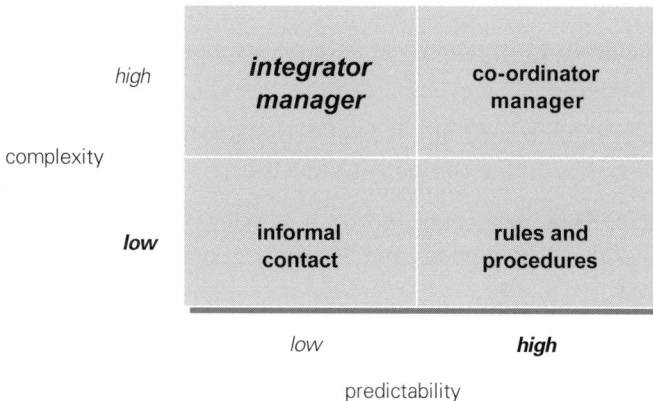

Figure 4: Guidelines for organising logistics management

Hands-on experience

A study has been conducted into experience with centralised logistical organisation. Decentralised logistical organisation is appropriate for situations involving low logistical complexity and high logistical predictability. This leads to consistently solid logistical performance. If a company that faces high logistical complexity and logistical predictability opts for decentralised logistical organisation, its logistical performance cannot be effective. The question then becomes whether a centralised logistical organisation is appropriate for situations involving high logistical complexity and low logistical predictability. Actual practice demonstrates that this is not necessarily the case. Although companies that opted to centrally organise logistics management initially improved logistical performance, this performance improvement could not be maintained. The question of whether a centralised logistical organisation is appropriate in situations involving high logistical complexity and low logistical predictability cannot simply be answered positively.

Possible explanations for the lack of actual success of centralised logistical organisation can be found in the following (Ploos van Amstel, 2002):

- It is questionable whether it is possible to achieve consistently sound logistical performance in situations involving high logistical complexity and low logistical predictability

- The inability to maintain a focus on and priority for logistics.

- Effecting centralised organisation of logistics management all at once, rather than in phases.

- Insufficiently rapid results and lack of demonstrable proof of the positive impact of logistics on the company's objectives.

- An insufficiently sophisticated approach to delegating logistical decisions at the level of the flow of goods and at departmental level.

5. Logistical organisation in ILC

Now that it is clear how the organisation of logistics management is viewed inside companies, the question shifts to how logistics organisations must be viewed when they cross company boundaries, as is the case with ILC. ILC also involve a number of organisational problems. Consider the example of Distrivaart. There are a number of questions at the strategic level including: Who determines the design of the distribution network? Who determines the investments in ships and dock interfaces? Who determines how the operation costs are to be divided among the parties involved? Questions at the tactical level include: Who selects the parties for road transport? Who determines the service schedule? How is the capacity divided among the parties? Finally, questions at operational level include: What stock is assigned to what client? What products will be the first to be unloaded and supplied to the retailer's distribution centre? What stock is held? By which ships? These are just a few of the many logistical decisions that need to be taken.

ILC are typically found in logistically complex and unpredictable environments. At first glance, centralised logistical organisation seems the right way to have proper control and achieve greater transparency. The well-known 'orchestrator' enters the scene. This is, however, a sensitive point in implementing ILC. This organisational issue leads to the question of who is in charge of the chain and, consequently, determines consumer satisfaction. Centralised supply chain management offers substantial co-ordination potential, leads to improved use of capacity and is cost saving. But what must one do at the operational level? This entails choosing, for example, which client has priority, or which ship must be the first to be unloaded. These are decisions that have an immediate impact on the logistical performance of the shipper. For this reason, it is essential to take a nuanced approach to the organisational question. There are a lot of pitfalls in centralising logistics management at company level but also, and even more so, in terms of inter-organizational co-ordination. The question then arises as to whether the complete centralisation of operational stock management at Akzo Nobel was perhaps too extreme.

Logistics management plays a decisive role in the success of ILC. A large number of decisions are taken at various levels (strategic, tactical and operational). Together, strategic and tactical processes can be effectively planned from a collaborative perspective. In terms of logistical organisation: centralised planning.

Operational co-ordination should take place at as low a level in the organisation as possible (i.e. decentralised implementation). The advantages of a decentralised organisation previously identified are of key importance. The decision-making process is faster, leading to a more efficient and effective organisation. Decentralisation enables parties to respond immediately to changing conditions. This, however, means that the supply chain parties involved must initially work together to improve predictability and reduce complexity, primarily through effective strategic and tactical planning. Otherwise a centralised logistical supply chain organisation and operational decision-making are inevitable, with all the associated problems.

The operational level has clout. Decentralised organisation requires a number of points to be taken into consideration. Continuous improvisation can ultimately result in a reduced level of service and increased costs. This then increases the tendency to centralization. Supply chain performance must be transparent. One must be able to learn from improvisation. This helps reduce complexity and increase predictability. The ability to learn must be developed at both the strategic and the tactical level (i.e. Plan Do Check Act (PDCA)). Operations must therefore be decentrally organised wherever possible, but it is essential to establish: Who has a say in what? Who has decision-making authority? Who needs to be informed? Regarding what issues? Who is responsible for tracking and tracing? Who is responsible for the correct information? This may be achieved using such approaches as the one proposed by ex-Cisco logistics manager Niek Visarius (i.e. the five Ps – perfect preparation prevents poor performance).

The logistics manager and the organisation

What does this mean for the traditional logistics manager present in many companies? For a logistics manager with a strong focus on centralisation who in the future must be able perform in an ILC context, it is essential that a move be made from internal logistics to external logistics. A successful supply chain demands perfectly co-ordinated logistics of several parties. In situations where company boundaries are transcended, most of the decisions are taken by operational employees; management shares information regarding company strategy and performance, employees are encouraged and managers ensure that everyone works to achieve the same objectives. To cross external boundaries, managers of a 'boundaryless' company focus on maximising the value for the end client in the supply chain, seek collaboration and partnerships based on trust, and spend the most time with clients, suppliers and other supply chain parties (Ashkenas et al., 1996).

6. Summary and conclusion

The future is in ILC – improved client satisfaction in return for optimal efforts in the supply chain through collaboration, transparency and use of information. Logistics management plays a decisive role in the success of ILC. The network may be highly sophisticated and ICT advanced, but planning and management ultimately determine effectiveness and efficiency. The question of logistical organisation may not be shunned. A centralised organisation is usually the first option to be considered. The authors, however, feel that a more sophisticated approach is necessary. Centralised logistical organisation in ILC entails far more pitfalls than those already associated with a centralised logistical organisation within a company. Decentralised organisation is favoured. This determines clout, but also demands that all supply chain parties work to improve the logistical complexity and predictability at the strategic and the tactical level. If daily operational complexity is high and predictability low, then a centralised logistical organisation and all the risks it entails seem inevitable. In short, the organisational expert perspective is relevant in assessing the successes and failures of ILC.

7. References

Ashkenas, R./Ulrich, D./Jick, T./Kerr, S. (1995), *The boundaryless organisation*, Jossey-Bass Inc., San Francisco.

Bertrand, J.W.M. (1988), "Logistieke beslissingen in de bedrijfsvoering" (Logistical decisions in company operations), Bedrijfskunde, 60, 1988/1, pp. 4-10. [Kluwer Bedrijfswetenschappen, Deventer.]

Christopher, M. (1998), *Logistics and supply chain management*, Financial Times/Prentice Hall, Hearthrow.

Fisher, M.L. (1997), "What is the right supply chain for your products?" Harvard Business Review, March/April 1997.

Galbraith, J.R. (2000), *Designing the global corporation*, Jossey-Bass, San Francisco.

Goor, A.R. van (2002), "Integraal customer service concept" (Integrated customer service concept), Tijdschrift voor Inkoop & Logistiek, 7, 1991/10, pp. 40-46. [Kluwer Bedrijfswetenschappen, Deventer]

Goor, A.R. van/Ploos van Amstel, M.J./Ploos van Amstel, W. (2003), *European distribution and supply chain logistics*, Educatieve Partners, Groningen.

Merriënboer, S.A./Vermunt, A.J.M./Voskuilen, M.J.M. (2002), "Transparantie: noodzaak of gevaar voor defensie" (Transparency: necessity or threat to defence), Militaire Spectator, 171, 2002/11.

Mintzberg, H. (1993), *Organisatiestructuren* (Dutch translation of 'Structures in five: designing effective organisation'), Prentice Hall Academic Service, Schoonhoven.

Ploos van Amstel, W. (2002), *Het organiseren van logistieke beheersing* (Organising logistics management), Lemma, Utrecht.

Vries, J. de (1999), *Logistiek organiseren* (Logistical organisation), Van Denderen, Groningen.

Wit, P. de/Verduijn, T. (2001), *Intelligente logistieke concepten: concepten, mogelijkheden, implementatie en ervaringen* (Intelligent logistics concepts: concepts, possibilities, implementation and experience), TNO Inro/NDL, Delft.

4.

Hub to Higher Performance?
An Internet Hub for the Vos Logistics Supply Chain

Jos van Hillegersberg, Jimmy Tseng, Rob Zuidwijk,
Marcel van Oosterhout, Jo van Nunen
(Erasmus University Rotterdam)

Abstract

Sharing information between multiple parties in a multi-modal logistics chain can potentially improve co-ordination within the chain. However, information sharing also requires the participation and collaboration of multiple parties whose goals are not always aligned with each other. This chapter describes experiences from the ongoing implementation of a Logistics Hub system for a transport chain directed by Vos Logistics. Interviews with participants in the logistics chain were conducted to analyse the Hub, its implementation process, and its effect on performance of the supply chain.

1. Introduction

Effective management of supply chains is a key element for firms seeking world-class performance (Davis, 1993). Firms today are expected to provide ever faster and more agile order-to delivery cycles. Parties in the supply chain are expected to improve efficiency in terms of reduction of waste and unit cost, compress time between order and delivery, and respond flexibly to orders (Brewer and Speh, 2000). Facing such competitive pressures, firms are looking beyond the boundaries of their organisations for performance. By collaborating with other parties in a supply chain, a firm seeks improvements beyond what is currently possible without collaboration. In fact, managing this type of collaboration and the challenges it raises is the essence of supply chain management.

Sharing information between multiple parties in a multi-modal logistics chain is a case in point. Access to accurate location and status information in a timely manner can potentially improve co-ordination within the logistics chain. A wide array of ICT solutions has been suggested, ranging from information hubs to electronic markets. Although we have witnessed substantial investment into these solutions, little recent research is available that reports on actual experiences of designing and implementing a logistics Hub and assessing its effect on supply chain performance. This chapter addresses these issues using the Vos hub as an example.

1.1. The Vos Logistics Hub project

Vos Logistics[1] is a third party logistics service provider that is active in adding value to its portfolio of logistics services. Vos is one of the larger, asset based, transport and logistical companies on the European market. The company employs more than 4000 people working at more than 30 offices throughout Europe. The firm's long-term strategy is to become a full logistics service provider for its customers, offering services such as warehousing, transportation management and supply chain (re-)design.

This study is concerned with the Vos sea containers transport from its Veendam terminal to the Rotterdam harbour for customers such as Avebe, Domo, Friesland Dairy Foods, Kappa, Akzo and Dow Chemical. Dependent on the cost and speed requirements of the customer, transport takes place over road, water and rail connections. Several parties are involved in the supply chain such as rail operators, barge operators, charters, terminals etc. Although the use of multi-modal transport and multiple parties provides potential flexibility and efficiency, the management of the supply chain is more complicated. A study by KPMG (2000) reported that timely information to monitor and improve the Veendam-Rotterdam supply chain was lacking. Several parties relied on manual administration of container status information. Telephone and fax were used for numerous ordering processes. Furthermore, the diversity of parties involved made a quick introduction of an EDI standard unlikely. These factors inhibited tracking and tracing of containers throughout the transportation chain. Early 2000, Vos and Informore, an ICT company that specializes in providing logistics hubs, initiated a project to create a logistics information hub[2] that would improve monitoring and management of the Veendam-Rotterdam supply chain. Connekt decided to fund the project as part of the Research Program on Intelligent Logistics Concepts. The original project goals stated were (Connekt, 2000):

---

[1] Vos Logistics will be called Vos in the remainder of this chapter. For more information on Vos see http://www.voslogistics.com/

[2] The Logistics Hub developed by Informore for the Vos Logistics Veendam-Rotterdam supply chain will be simply called "the Hub" in this remainder of this chapter.

1. develop a showcase for co-ordination of transportation chains. Prove feasibility of a Hub as alternative for EDI standardization. Disseminate knowledge to other transportation chains.

2. provide increased efficiency and effectiveness of the supply chain through timely information exchange

3. facilitate a chain-director role for Vos, allowing Vos to serve as a logistics service provider for its customers

4. through a chain director role for Vos, compensate for the increased power of the shipping lines (aggregate information on large volumes of containers)

5. improve planning by parties in the chain, through more timely information and status messages. Reduce waiting times, increase throughput, etc.

1.2. The research project

While implementation of the Hub was proceeding, Connekt by the beginning of 2002 requested the Erasmus University Rotterdam/Faculteit Bedrijfskunde to conduct a study on the design, implementation process, expected/realized benefits, and future directions of the Hub. As this chapter goes to press, both the Hub implementation and the research project are ongoing. This chapter should thus be viewed as an intermediate report of our research findings. For conducting the research we focus on five main questions (Table 1).

No	Question	Chapter section
1	What information, financial and logistics processes take place in the Vos supply chain?	2
2	How will processes change and what performance improvements are expected/realized as a result of the hub?	3
3	How can the hub be positioned to alternative solutions for supply chain co-ordination?	4
4	What are success factors for implementing a hub for supporting transport chains?	5
5	What future developments are needed to ensure sustainable success of the Hub?	6

Table 1: Research questions

Our approach in addressing these questions includes literature study, two rounds of semi-structured interviews with the supply chain parties involved and Informore, analysis of the hub software design and of actual operational data after the hub goes into operation. The first round consisted of seven semi-structured interviews in five organisations participating in the Hub. A second round of interviews will be conducted as the participants start to use the Hub (anticipated by the end of November 2002).

An analysis of the current supply chain processes and the changes as a result of the hub (Question 1) is needed as a basis. We included questions in the interviews on current processes, systems and communications among parties.

To address performance improvements (Question 2), a research instrument was designed to track the changes after the Hub rollout. We identified performance indicators by asking the interviewees to elaborate on the performance indicators they believe to be relevant to their own organization for the management of logistics processes at the strategic level, the tactical level, and the operational level. Where available, quantitative data on these performance indicators will be collected and analysed. This will allow us to monitor the difference in performance of various logistics and information processes before and after the implementation of the Hub.

A positioning and precise definition of the Hub (Question 3) is needed to be able to apply earlier research findings to the Vos hub. It is also needed to address possible generalization of our research findings to other supply chain integration projects. To position the hub we use classification frameworks from the literature on inter-organisational systems (IOS) and enterprise application integration (EAI).

To address success factors for implementation (Question 4) we searched the literature on IOS implementation processes and discussed this topic with the parties during the interviews. Additional questions in the second round will focus on the implementation issues and the barriers to collaboration.

The future development directions of the Hub (Question 5) were also discussed in the interviews.

As this chapter goes to press, the first round of interviews and literature review have been completed (see figure 1). The Hub is expected to be in operation by November 2002. A number of inward adapters (to enable automatic confirmation messages to the Hub) need to be finalized and discussions on pricing agreements are still ongoing. This chapter thus represents an intermediate set of research results. However, the results of the first scan already include several interesting findings and lessons learned.

Research project

Hub architecture analysis

Literature study

Hub operational
Data analysis

Research   Phase 1   Phase 2
project   First round   Second round
initiated   Of interviews   of interviews

live

```
2000              2001              2002              2003
```

project   design and development   outward   inward   pricing
initiated   adapters   adapters contract
                                                                        agreements

Development project

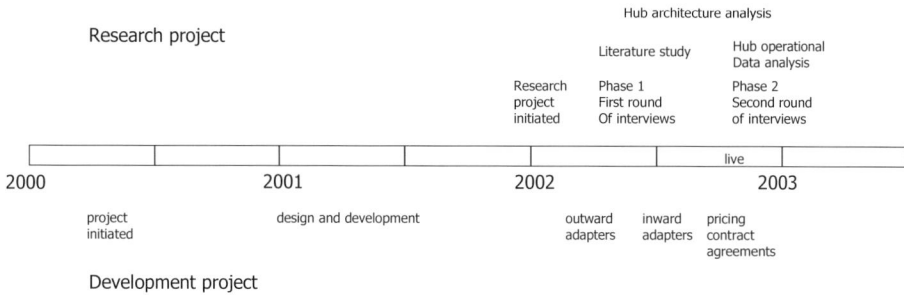

Figure 1: timing and activities of the hub development and research project

1.3. Outline of the chapter

The remaining sections of the chapter address the five research questions sequentially. Section 2 describes the current Vos container transport chain. Section 3, positions and analyses the hub using existing frameworks from IOS and EAI literature. Section 4 develops a framework for assessing performance improvement logistics chains as a result of a hub. Section 5 highlights some of the implementation issues identified. Section 6 presents conclusions and describes long-term prospects.

2. The current Vos Veendam-Rotterdam chain

The logistics chain in this case involves the transport (export) of maritime containers from a hinterland terminal in Veendam (Northern part of the Netherlands) through the port of Rotterdam, using a combination of transport modes (train, barge, truck). Multi-modal transport has certain advantages (e.g. price, environmental friendliness), but also requires additional handling of containers from one transport mode to the other. In particular, many organizations are involved in the physical transport of maritime containers (shippers, carriers, forwarders, etc.), and even more in information and value flows around the transport process (banks, insurance companies, customs, etc.). The scope of the research project is the transport chain from Vos Veendam to the shipping lines departing from the Rotterdam harbour. We describe in this section the current physical and information flows in some detail and some of the limits of the current situation.

2.1. Current physical flows

In figure 2 the main arrow represents a simplified image of the physical container flow and financial flows. In reality, many variations on this flow can occur. The container flow directed by Vos between Veendam and Rotterdam involves about 100 full containers daily. At the same time, a similar number of empty containers are moved from Rotterdam to Veendam to replenish the container stock in Veendam. For simplicity of exposition, we shall not discuss the flow of empty containers in this chapter. We also do not discuss multi-modal planning of containers on barge/truck/train, as the first operation of the Hub focuses on the train transport.

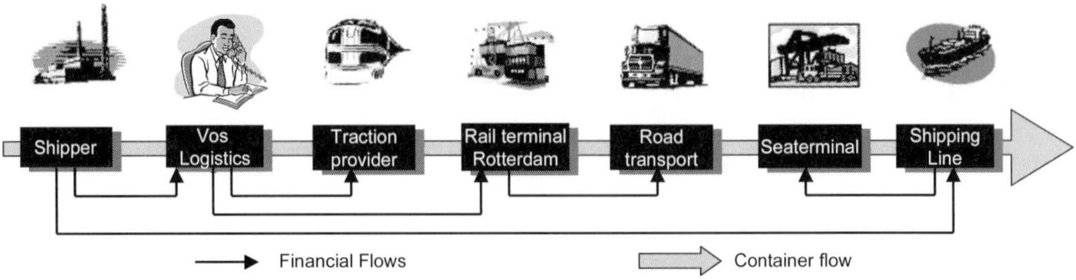

Figure 2: Current financial flows in the chain

A train shuttle transports full containers between Veendam and Rotterdam on a daily schedule. Currently, Vos batches its daily shipments into one daily trainload. The train shuttle to and from Veendam is managed by the train operator (ACTS) and its load capacity is booked by Vos at an earlier stage. The trigger for starting transport and information processes in the Vos chain is a transport order by a shipper to Vos. After having received a customer order, the Vos planning department plans the entire route to Rotterdam including the timeframe of this order and the operators that will be involved. The process has been slightly simplified since we have not shown the retrieval of an empty container from a depot to a shipper. Once the shipper has loaded an empty container with his goods, the full container is transported by truck (Vos Trucking) to Veendam, where RSC Groningen puts it on the train shuttle.

    The train shuttle goes to RSC Rotterdam Waalhaven, where the trainload is split, depending on the destination terminal in and around Rotterdam (ECT home terminal, ECT Delta terminal, etc.). Containers with destination ECT Delta Terminal stay on the train to the Maasvlakte. Containers with destination ECT Home Terminal are unloaded and transported with ECT internal transport. For other destinations, a trucking company (Peeman) is chartered by RSC Rotterdam to do final transport. After arriving at the sea terminal, containers are put onto the destination ship.

2.2. Current financial flows

The financial flows depicted in Figure 2 consist of invoices that indicate supplier-customer relationships. RSC-Rotterdam plays a role in co-ordinating between the truckers in the logistics chain, communicating with Peeman and ECT. Vos also sends messages to these parties (via fax and e-mail), but the communication between RSC-R and these parties is more extensive. This may be explained by the fact that RSC is commercially and financially inter-related with these parties. In contrast, there are no financial flows between Vos and these parties. Vos pays a fee to RSC for its co-ordination services. Although a party like ECT is an important link in the transport chain, it primary has a business relationship with the sea carrier.

2.3. Current information flows

As mentioned earlier, the trigger for starting the information flows is a transport order sent to Vos. The communication medium of this message varies per customer (generally fax, email or phone). Planning of the entire route and the involved transport providers is done at the Vos planning department. Vos collects all individual customer orders during the day and batches them into one EDI-message to RSC containing the data of the complete train load with detailed information at container level (container load, destination ship, the planned route for that container, the involved transport operators, and some other information). Between RSC-Rotterdam and the other parties in Rotterdam, communication takes place to co-ordinate the transport from the Rail terminal to the final destinations of the containers.

Prior to the implementation of the Hub, as can be seen in figure 3, the majority of the activities are co-ordinated using a combination of telephone and fax messages. EDI is used between RSC and the deep-sea terminal (ECT), and ECT and the sea carrier (P&O). Also, there is EDI communication between Vos and Rail Service Center Rotterdam (RSC-R) using a standard bilaterally agreed upon. To ensure delivery of the message, a 3rd party message forwarding service is used that charges a small fee per message.

Veendam – Rotterdam Current situation

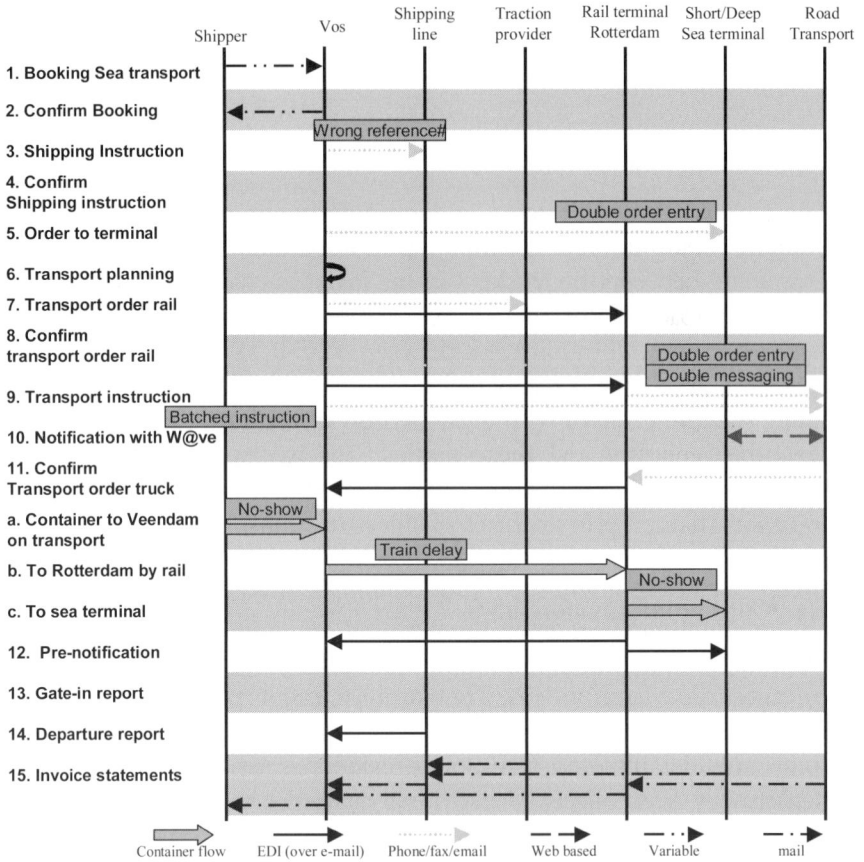

	Shipper	Vos	Shipping line	Traction provider	Rail terminal Rotterdam	Short/Deep Sea terminal	Road Transport

1. Booking Sea transport

2. Confirm Booking

Wrong reference#

3. Shipping Instruction

4. Confirm Shipping instruction

Double order entry

5. Order to terminal

6. Transport planning

7. Transport order rail

8. Confirm transport order rail

Double order entry
Double messaging

9. Transport instruction

Batched instruction

10. Notification with W@ve

11. Confirm Transport order truck

No-show

a. Container to Veendam on transport

Train delay

b. To Rotterdam by rail

No-show

c. To sea terminal

12. Pre-notification

13. Gate-in report

14. Departure report

15. Invoice statements

Container flow   EDI (over e-mail)   Phone/fax/email   Web based   Variable   mail

Figure 3: Current Veendam-Rotterdam information flows and sample problems

2.4. Current limitations of physical and information processes

The current information process results in several limitations. Figure 3 illustrates some of these. Currently, Vos sends a load list of the planned trainload 24 hours before the train arrival in Rotterdam, but the message with the actual train-load is often sent only 4-5 hours before arrival of the train in Rotterdam. Especially for the planning of further transport at the other involved transport providers, earlier notification would be beneficial.

No real-time information about the status of containers is available. There is no comprehensive system for tracking the containers in the current logistics chain. Current status information is unreliable because it depends on parties in different stages of automation, and it is not timely because it is based on batch-based processing of EDI messages.

A large number of containers are involved in exceptions. Examples of exceptions are: delays of train arrival at the train terminal, "no-shows" of containers while loading a train, and administrative problems concerning references to containers or bookings. Although usually enough time slack is available in the chain, any type of delay results in additional (administrative) effort. To illustrate, up to 10% of the containers on the train load list cannot be loaded before the critical departure time resulting in "no shows" and a negative impact on the train utilization rate. These "no-shows" may be due to the lack of accurate information (inaccurate references) or containers that are still not physically present at the critical departure time. A container can be delayed because a trucker is unable to retrieve the specified container from the empty container depot. These errors would then propagate throughout the chain, disrupting action plans, and requiring extensive human intervention through telephone and fax messages to rectify. Re-scheduling cannot take place until the source of the error can be identified. This is not always easy to accomplish without up-to-date status information.

Although the transport of containers seems simple, many parties are involved, and many pieces of information from these parties need to be consolidated at the right place at the right time in order to avoid operational problems. For this reason, it is not surprising that "normal business" is disrupted by "exceptions". Furthermore, in the current situation, the information processing activities suffer from duplicate order entries, that result in errors, and reduced transparency as status information is not shared frequently enough in order to avoid discrepancies due to local updates etc. It is clear that either avoiding exceptions or standardizing exception handling (seemingly a contradictio in terminis), will result in cost benefits. We will address such issues and potential improvement in more detail in section 3. First we will introduce the Hub for the Vos supply chain designed by Informore.

2.5. The Hub architecture

Figure 4 depicts the high level architecture of the Informore Hub system. The main application implemented for parties in this logistics chain is a transport scenario and route/leg management system. The route/leg management system defines and stores information on transport routes serviced by different transport partners. Pre-arranged contracts with business partners and subcontractors are stored as transport scenarios and business rules. Tariffs, locations, transport modes and transit times are determined for each route. A comparison function allows planners to calculate alternative scenarios in order to chose the easiest, the cheapest or the quickest route available. The transport scenario management system manages bookings and transport orders in the logistics chain. A transport manager would use the transport scenario and route management system to initiate a booking or transport order, which in turn initiates information exchange between the relevant parties. These transactions then trigger actions and notifications based on the transport scenario and business rules for that transaction. The user-interface is customized for the various parties in the chain. The attributes shown and the access rights (view, update, delete) are tailored towards their needs.

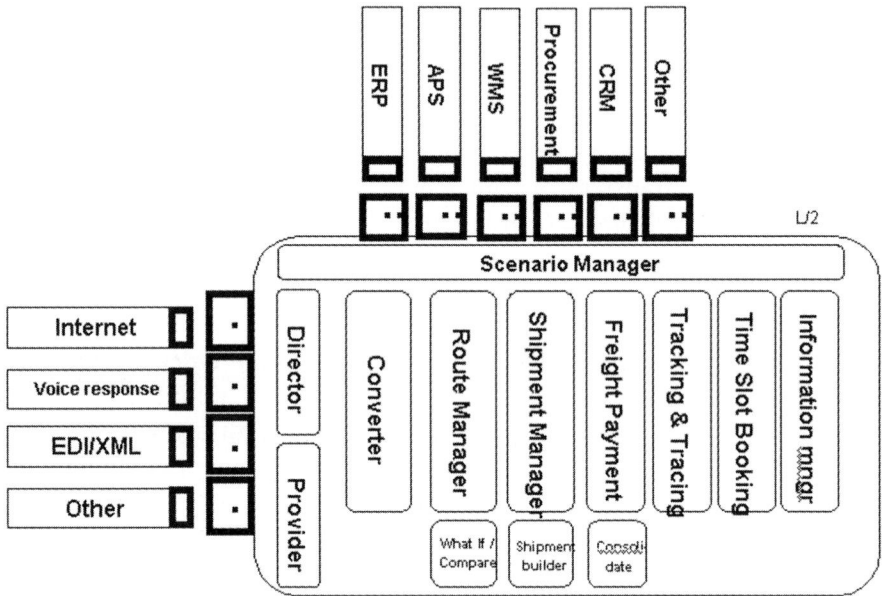

Figure 4: the Hub architecture (source Informore, 2002)

Using the Hub, the chain director (Vos) can monitor the information exchange and the activities taking place on a "real-time" basis. Other parties connected can monitor part of the information in the hub of interest to them. The hub supports various standards, but is also designed to support proprietary message formats through custom-built adapters. Section 4.4 will elaborate on this. The Informore hub comes with a web-browser based user-interface that is designed for monitoring, planning and demo purposes. However, the built-in user-interface was not designed to support high-volume data entry. In the next section we discuss how the Hub enables changes in processes and how performance improvement can be measured.

Veendam - Rotterdam Datahub full rollout

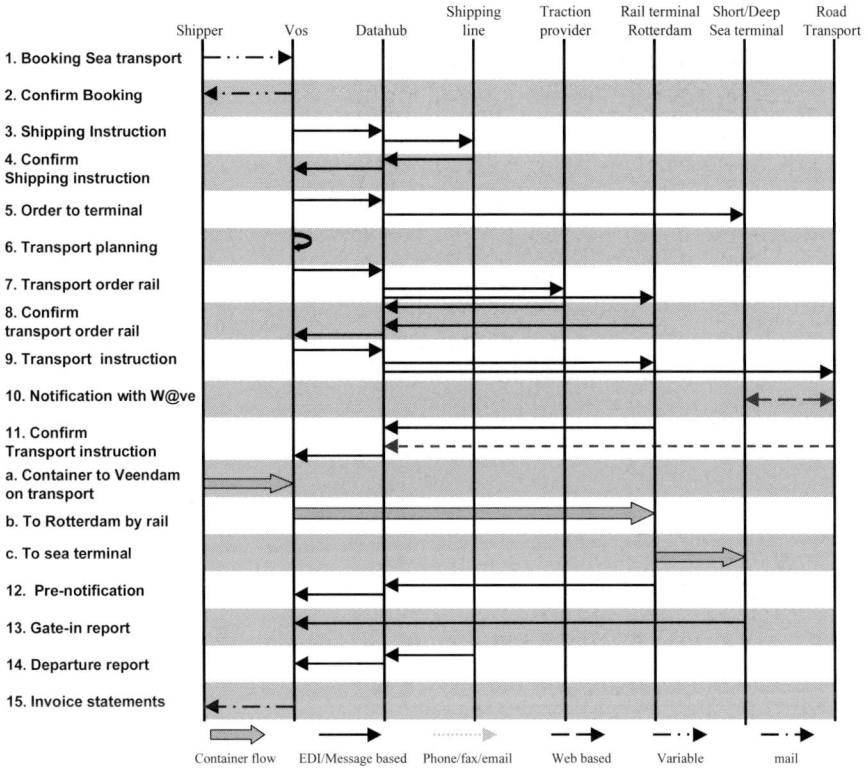

Figure 5: expected improvements after Hub implementation

3. Performance improvement with the Hub

3.1. Information processes after implementation of the Hub

Figure 5 illustrates the situation after the Hub goes into operation. Note that most information processes now go through the hub. Only the road transport (Overbeek) will use the web-interface for data entry and monitoring. All others will communicate through EDI messages (technical details in section 4). The figure only shows the main information flows. Any party can go at any time to the web-interface when specific information is needed, e.g. to monitor a container status in the case of an exception. To assess how to measure performance improvement, the next sections identify performance indicators relevant to parties in the chain.

3.2. Identifying Performance Indicators

Several frameworks have been introduced to provide performance metrics not only for individual firms, but also for supply chains. Brewer and Speh (2000) propose a framework based on the balanced scorecard. Lambert and Pohlen (2001) propose a framework based on profit and loss statements. Conkins (2001) proposes a framework based on activity-based costing. Unfortunately, there is no generally accepted framework for supply chain measurement. In the absence of such a framework, supply chain metrics have traditionally been defined in terms of internal logistics performance (Lambert and Pohlen, 2001). The focus on internal logistics performance reflects the difficulty in measuring performance, and the lack of chain wide orientation. This often presents an impediment to collaboration within a chain.

ECT – Deep Sea Terminal	Peeman – Road Transport
1.Timeliness of information	11.Order processing time
2.Quality of information received messages	12.Quality of information, error rate
3.No-show rate of containers on arriving trains	13.Timeliness of received information
4.Punctuality of train arrivals	14.Truck utilization
5.Throughput time of containers at terminal	
RSC-Rotterdam – Train Terminal	**Vos Logistics Service Provider**
6.Train load planning vs. realization	15.Train utilization
7.Throughput time of trucks at terminal	16.Waiting time at terminals
8.Punctuality of train arrivals	17.Loading time
9.Quality of EDI messages	18.Quality of information
10.Number of operators that send EDI messages	19.Timeliness of information
	20.Chain transparency

Table 2: Sample category of performance indicators mentioned in interviews

Following the tradition of exploratory case studies, we identify performance indicators by asking the interviewees to elaborate on the performance indicators they believe to be relevant to their own organisation for the management of logistics processes (see Table 2). In the interviews with RSC and ECT, some performance indicators were mentioned that are less relevant to co-ordination issues. For RSC this is safety and the damage rate, for ECT it is crane performance. A number of remarks concerning the performance indicators are in order here:

-   *Multiple parties recognize the same performance indicators.* For example, the punctuality of train arrivals at the terminal is recognized as an important PI explicitly by ECT and RSC-Rotterdam. When several parties are involved, it becomes relevant to state who 1) is responsible for the outcome of the performance, 2) sets the standards, 3) is responsible for measuring performance and maintaining performance data. Responsibility of chain performance usually lies in the hands of several parties. Indeed, a late train arrival may be caused by delays in operation at the origin rail terminal, or during rail transport. The delay may also be caused by untimely information delivery by other parties. This makes the first issue complicated. The standard is set by the customer or in this case, the planner (arrival time). The arrival time is measured at the rail terminal.

-   *Performance indicators are at different management levels.* Some performance indicators (punctuality, throughput times) are at an operational level, and can be measured quantitatively. Others (number of operators that use EDI messages) are at a more tactical or strategic level, and constitute with other aspects the relationship between two organizations.

3.3.   Information processing benefits

In this section, we group expected benefits from the Hub (see Section 2) using the performance indicators put forward by the companies (Section 3.2, Table 2). We shall denote performance indicators e.g. with numbers 4 and 7 in Table 2 by (PI-4,7).

Increase of administrative productivity and efficiency. Administrative effort relates to the time and resources that are required to co-ordinate the logistical flow (e.g. order entry and processing per customer). In the current situation, several parties in the Vos chain (e.g. Peeman) are forced to do a re-entry of the order information into their internal systems because they receive their information by e-mail or fax. Duplicate order entry results in lower productivity and may cause higher error rates. Furthermore, in the current situation much effort (telephone, fax) has to be done between chain members to recover missing information and errors, which has a negative impact on productivity and henceforth on (cost) efficiency. Implementation of the Hub will make re-entry of orders redundant and may streamline exception handling.

Chain transparency (PI-20) can be defined as the ability to provide accurate and up-to-date information for parties to co-ordinate activities within the logistics chain (e.g. the level of detail on location and status information, the timeliness of notifying other parties for planning purposes). In other words, chain transparency enables better performance. In the current situation, Vos is using a batched order processing system. The chain partners are not informed in real time about the transport orders for the next day (PI-1,13,19), but in a batched trainload list at the end of the day. This causes difficulties for their planning systems and those of transport operators responsible for additional transport. As soon as information emerges somewhere in the chain that is useful for other chain members, that information should be made visible real time throughout the whole chain. The Hub could be a useful tool to get more transparency in the chain, but in several interviews (ECT, RSC, Peeman) the remark was made that "more information does not always make you happier"(C. Hoenders of RSC). Although EDI connections are considered valuable (PI-10), the Hub may have additional value if it enables alert messaging.

Chain co-ordination can be defined as the ability to synchronize activities between different parties in the chain (e.g. the timely release of containers from a terminal). As such, chain co-ordination does not merely concern the punctuality of individual processes, but also the synchronization in (re-) planning of these processes (PI-6). Despite the remarks in the interviews of the danger of information overkill in the Hub, the interviewed chain members agreed that a good exception and alert messaging system could be very useful for this chain. A container can be delayed because a trucker is unable to retrieve the specified container from the empty container depot. These errors would then propagate throughout the chain, disrupting action plans, and requiring extensive human intervention through telephone and fax messages to rectify. Re-scheduling cannot take place until the source of the error has been identified. This is not always easy to accomplish without up-to-date status information.

Increase of customer satisfaction. Customer satisfaction can be defined as the extent to which the perceived logistics performance of contractee matches the expectations of contractor. In the performance measurement framework, this will be measured in terms of service levels. At the current stage in the Hub project, we have not yet interviewed a customer of Vos, but we expect indicators to be important such as timeliness of container arrival, and quality of tracking and tracing information.

3.4. Logistics benefits

On the short term, implementation of the Hub will have certain administrative benefits, as explained in Section 3.3. In addition, if the information is used to streamline logistics processes, logistics benefits can also be identified.

Shorter chain throughput time. Chain throughput time can be defined as the time required to deliver from the source of the logistics chain to the destination (e.g. port to door, door to door). Logistics throughput time does not merely require acceleration of individual processes, but also improved co-ordination between chain members (in order to avoid waiting times). One process that depends considerably on co-ordination is multi-modal transition. The time required to switch from one transport mode to another (PI-5,7,16,17) depends on loading and unloading time at the rail terminal (PI-16), but also on the time a train must wait before it can be loaded or unloaded.

Better resource utilization. A critical performance indicator for Vos is the train utilization rate (PI-6,15). Up to 10% of the containers on the train load list of the Vos shuttle cannot be loaded before the critical departure time, resulting in a negative impact on the train utilization rate. These "no-shows" (PI-3) may be due to the lack of accurate information (inaccurate references) or containers that are still not physically present at the critical departure time.

Higher resource productivity. Waiting times of e.g. trucks have a negative impact on the productivity of these resources (PI-14). Punctuality of train arrivals (PI-4,8) is an important issue, as many resources (cranes, trucks) will have to wait if the train does not arrive on schedule.

Chain wide monitoring and improvement. As will be discussed in more detail in section 4, an IOS can have several levels of functionality. At the first level, chain members get connected. Next, the information interchange between chain members could support the operational activities, for example better co-ordination of activities. In the final stage, an IOS system could generate input for management information, a chain wide performance monitoring system (PI-20). At the moment of this publication, the parties involved are mainly at the connectivity level. During the pilot, the opportunities for the Hub to generate input for a chain monitoring system will be assessed. For instance, using gate-in and gate-out status messages it becomes feasible to generate chain wide throughput time reports. In addition, error reports can be retrieved from the hub data.

The absence of chain-wide performance indicators makes it difficult to orchestrate collective efforts aimed at chain-wide improvements. This will need to be addressed together with the proper incentives for collaboration. For instance, most parties are happy to receive more accurate and timely information, but are more reluctant to put the information there (if not yet acquired automatically) or to share it (if already available for other purposes).

4. Positioning the Hub

Already in 1971 Stern introduced the term Inter-organizational Information System (IOS). IOS cross organizational boundaries linking one or more firms to their customers and/or suppliers (Barett and Konsinsky, 1982). Golden & Powell (1999) stress the potential strategic advantage: "IOS are information systems that facilitate the exchange of information electronically using telecommunications between different organisations' computer systems and can be a mechanism for strategic advantage.". This strategic advantage includes flexibility. Flexibility can be technological, organisational, shared and network flexibility (Golden and Powell, 1999). Besides the increased flexibility, there may also be economic reasons for organisations to create an alliance or inter-firm co-operation between two or more organisations on information exchange such as sharing costs of large investment, reduction in supply-chain uncertainty, etc. (Clemons & Row, 1992; Culpan, 1993; Cilroy, 1993; Guglar & Dunning, 1993; Konsynski, 1993; van der Heijden et al., 1995).

However, too many different types of IOS exist to put forward any benefits, risks or success factors that apply in general. Therefore, a further typology of IOS is needed. Several authors have proposed classifications of IOS on varying dimensions. As argued by Alt and Klein (1998), a full understanding of IOS and their success factors can only be achieved by applying a multi-disciplinary approach. Both technology and organizational factors need to be considered. Therefore, in this section, we use organizational views (IOS, e-markets) and technological views (EAI) to position the Hub and explore its current position and growth potential.

4.1. Linkage view

Hong and Kim (1998) classify IOS into three main types: vertical, horizontal and cross IOS (see Figure 6). A horizontal IOS links a homogeneous group of organizations in order to foster their mutual co-operation. Incentives for horizontal IOS include scale economies in operations and horizontal market transactions. Also, the cost and skills required to implement IOS can be shared. An horizontal IOS typically reflects a market coalition or partnership. A vertical IOS links organizations that play different roles in a value chain. Vertical IOS typically support the value chain of an IOS participant. The more unique roles the participants play, the higher the vertical linkage. A cross IOS is an IOS that is both horizontally and vertically linked. Cross IOS enable benefits resulting from vertical co-operation combined with resource-oriented incentives of horizontal co-operation. A well known example of a cross IOS is Singapore Tradenet, an EDI system created by Singapore government to facilitate computer-to-computer exchange of inter-company using EDIFACT.

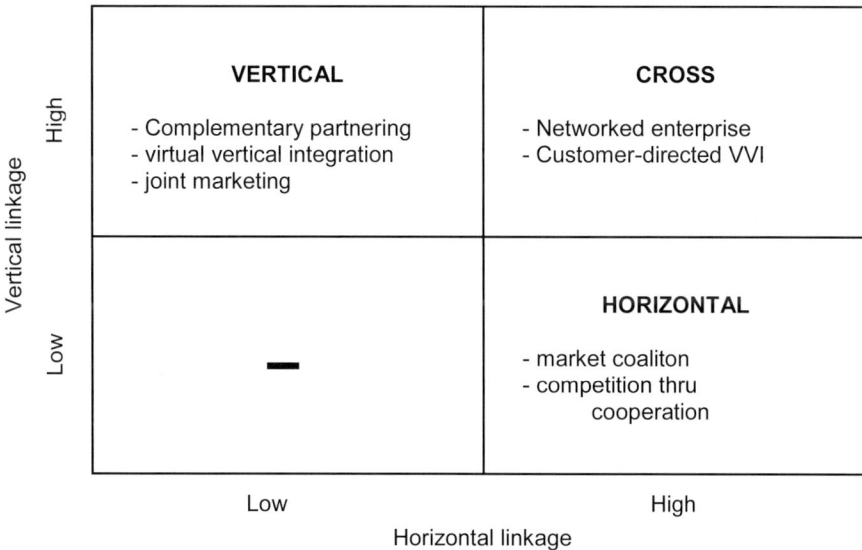

Figure 6: High level characterization of IOS (source: Hong and Kim, 1998)

The Vos hub, according to this classification, is a vertical IOS, mainly supporting the value chain of Vos. However, some horizontal linkages could be easily supported, as some of the parties play similar roles. E.g. several charters (Peeman, Vos trucking) are connected to the Hub. Also the train operator and barge operator offer similar services and may develop closer horizontal partnerships that are supported by the Vos Hub. Thus, in the near future the Hub could evolve into a cross-IOS, offering more strategic support for vertical collaboration and horizontal partnerships. Other than the Singapore Tradenet the Hub does not require document/message standardization. This lowers barriers for (low-tech) parties that wish to connect. The current design of the Vos Hub makes it a private vertical IOS. However, as will be discussed later in this section, the Hub can potentially evolve into a (public) cross IOS through connecting new parties, or by building links to other IOSs.

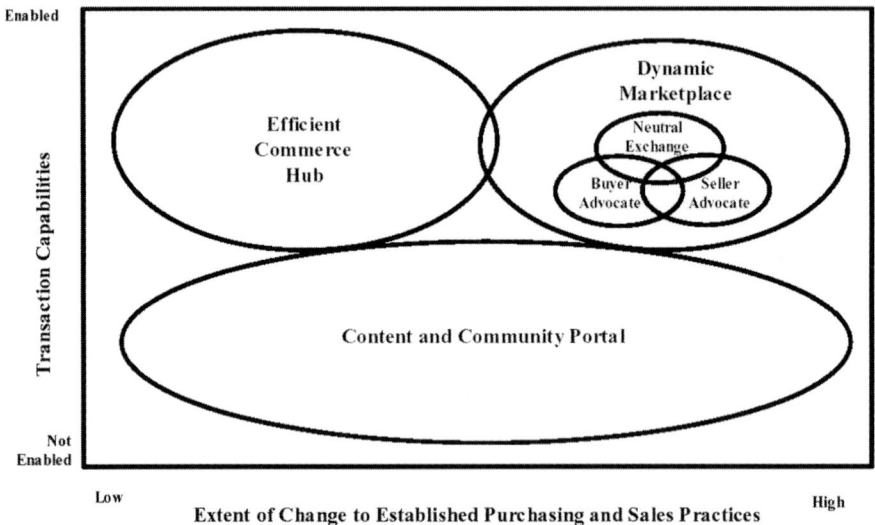

Figure 7: Functional categorization of E-markets (source Thomas, 2000)

4.2. Transaction and process change view

Thomas (2000) adapts a model from Gartner Group to describe three main types of E-markets, segmented based on their change potential to existing processes and transaction capabilities (see figure 7).

Content and community platforms do not offer transaction capabilities, but focus on community building and exchange of information. They can be used to publish information of joint interest, such as design drawings and buyer/supplier lists.

Dynamic marketplaces enable for dynamic negotiation regarding the terms of transaction, such as pricing, quality and delivery time. By offering several market making mechanisms (auctions, RFP/RFQ mechanisms) dynamic markets usually imply changes to the established practices in a market.

Efficient commerce hubs automate existing transaction flows aiming to increase efficiency. Hubs do not aim to change value chain relationships and pricing models, but attempt to eliminate underlying transaction inefficiencies. Examples of such inefficiencies include Error-prone manual processes, chapter-based supplier catalogs, inefficient direct or phone based sales staff, and general dearth of information in the supply chain. Hubs may perform on-line content management, product and availability transparency, automated requisition routing and approval, order matching, fulfilment, settlement and enable value-chain collaboration. Thomas notes that hubs usually provide 'limited integration' to trading partner's back-end systems. Thomas further observes that hubs do not offer sourcing alternatives nor pricing transparency and thus have limited impact to established purchasing and sales practices.

Hubs and Portals can be either *public* or *private*. In the case of a private marketplace a limited list of trading partners is included, usually based on the preference of important customers or suppliers. Typically private information hubs start small and grow slowly, but every improvement has sizeable potential to benefit participants (Garcia & Lambert, 2002 pp. 10). As private information hubs are lead by a chain director, its interests guide the growth of such a hub (e.g. add new suppliers to increase competition).

Using this perspective, the Vos Hub can be viewed as a private efficient e-commerce hub. The Hub is based on an information-sharing model in which a specialised logistics execution service provider maintains a database on behalf of participating organizations in the supply chain. Its current services are focused on systemizing and automating transactions between trade partners in the value chain. Back-end system integration provided by Hub will potentially reduce administrative costs (including phone, fax, chapter) and labor expenses, minimize errors, eliminate redundant orders. The Hub also could provide value chain visibility and collaboration. Once in full operation, it will hold all information needed to increase value chain visibility and process transparency. This could be a basis for supply chain business process management and optimization using decision support tools. The hub could provide a basis to evolve into a dynamic market and/or community portal. Currently pricing is fixed in long-term contracts. A more dynamic market model is only beneficial if the Hub would allow more trade partners enabling a choice of transport options. Currently the choice is limited to a multi-modal train/barge decision. Providers of various transport legs are fixed.

4.3. An interdependence view

Kumar and van Dissel (1996) introduce a three parts typology for IOSs based on the classification by Thompson (1967) of various types of interdependencies that exist among organisations (see figure 8):

Type of interdependence	Pooled interdependency	Sequential interdependency	Reciprocal interdependency
Configuration	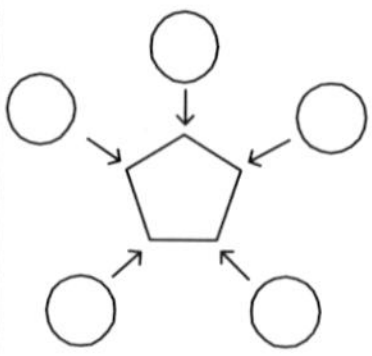		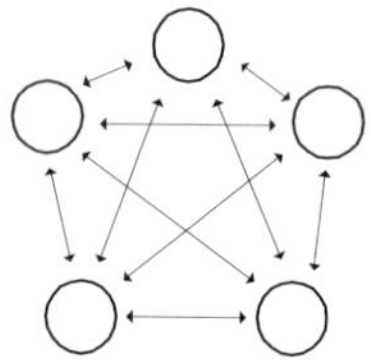

Figure 8: three types of IOS (adapted from Kumar and van Dissel, 1996)

IS/ICT resources such as databases, networks and applications are shared among organizations in pooled information resource IOSs. Shared systems such as hotel and airline reservation systems are examples of this type. The main drivers for pooled IOS are economies of scale including cost and risk sharing. The authors also characterize electronic markets as pooled IOS. Utilizing common standards and rules, electronic markets facilitate interorganizational transactions.

Value/supply chain IOS facilitate sequential interdependencies among supplier/customer in a value/supply chain. "These IOSs insitutionalize sequential interdependencies between organizations". Examples of sequential interaction include is EDI-based ordering and tracking and tracing of orders. The key motivators for value/supply chain IOS are achieving reduction of uncertainty, thereby achieving cost, cycle time and quality advantages over competing chains.

The third type, network IOS, operationalize reciprocal interdependencies. Organisations attempt to utilize each other's complementary capabilities, resulting in specific benefits for each party in the co-operation. The ICT use is usually unstructured tool support for (team) processes such as communication, design, negotiation and conflict resolution. Recent

Internet based groupware systems such as Eroom.com and Projectplace.com are used widely to create IOS for joint design and development.

The Hub system possesses characteristics of pooled and value/supply chain IOSs. The Hub itself contains a central database that is accessible for each organisation through a custom made adapter. This is a characteristic of pooled IOS. Through a mechanism of controlled create/read/update and delete (CRUD) rights, the various parties can share visibility of information that is of common interest. Hub is geographically located at Informore, a company specializing in IOS for logistics. Access to the Hub is provided over a standard secure Internet connection. Informore can be viewed as an Application Services Provider (ASP). Informore provides development, implementation, hardware and operation services to the Hub participants. Thus, these ICT resources and services are 'pooled'. Costs are billed per transaction (container) to Vos, who intends to partly relocate these costs to other organisations. By sharing the costs economies of scale could be achieved. At this point negotiations as to how much each party should contribute are still ongoing.

Other than Kumar and van Dissel suggest, the Hub is only partly standardized. The inability to implement standards within the transport sector is compensated by flexibility of the Hub system and custom developed adapters that link the Hub to the systems of the various participants. The Hub data-model accommodates for an 'integrated view' of all data that is of shared interest. Through user-defined fields it can be extended if needed. The adapters are custom built for each participant and it can be debated whether they are part of the 'shared pool of resources'. Currently debates are going on whether all parties should pay for an 'exotic' adapter needed as a result of a change in an internal system of one of the participants.

The recent technology of custom adapters thus reduces the need for standards. However, standards and procedures are needed to assure timely information updates in the Hub. The frequency and timing of information updates and confirmations should be agreed upon to achieve some of the original goals. It seems that these standard procedures have not been strictly agreed upon beforehand, and currently they are debated as they have impact on the administrative procedures in place.

The Hub also possesses characteristics of a value/supply chain IOS. Although its configuration resembles that of a 'pooled' IOS, the actual flow of information realized is mostly sequential. As the description of the current process shows the core process supported by Hub is sequential. Thus, the Hub automates the current sequential process through a 'pooled' configuration. The Hub goals are in line with those identified by Kumar and van Dissel, e.g. reduced cycle time, cost and improved quality. The Hub does not (yet) have properties of a networked IOS. The functionality of the Hub is mainly supply-chain execution. Currently no collaborative tools such as discussion groups, negotiation support, etc. are in place. Hub may in the future evolve into a networked IOS. We discuss this in the 6th section of this chapter.

4.4. A technology view

Parties in the supply chain access logistics services through a web-based interface or through interfaces that convert the data between the business systems and the Hub application. In this case, a logistics execution service provider pools the information resources into common information hub. Where electronic data is already available in one part of the logistics chain, the service provider provides adapters for converting the data between various business systems and the Hub application. Other parties in the supply chain access logistics services through a web-based interface.

Process integration		
Development services	**Process management services** ● Transformation coordination services	**Runtime services**
Object integration		
● Process modelling ● Transformation specification ● Interface development	**Transformation services** ● Identification and validation services ● Synchronization services ● Routing services ● Transaction processing services	● Distribution services ● Scalability services ● Monitoring services
Data integration		
	Connectivity services ● Communication services ● Addressing and delivery services ● Security services	**Interface services** ● Interface translation services ● Metadata representation services

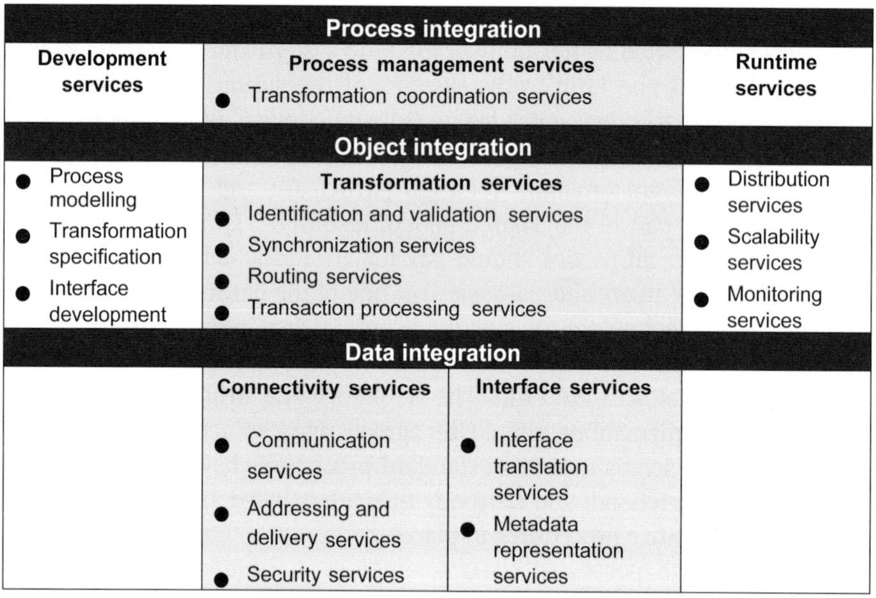

Figure 9: ICT services incorporated in IOS (source: Puschmann and Alt, 2001)

Puschmann and Alt (2001) propose three levels of integration and the corresponding services that should be included in the IOS (see figure 9).

Most current IOS enable data-integration and only deploy basic connectivity and interface services. Advanced IOS should allow flexible process integration and will achieve this by offering transformation and process management services.

Two basic principles behind the architecture of data sharing in inter-organizational information systems can be identified. The first is based on a collection of bilateral connections between the participating parties, the second uses a central node that connects to all parties involved (Figure 10).

Federated Architecture   **Hub-and-spoke Architecture**

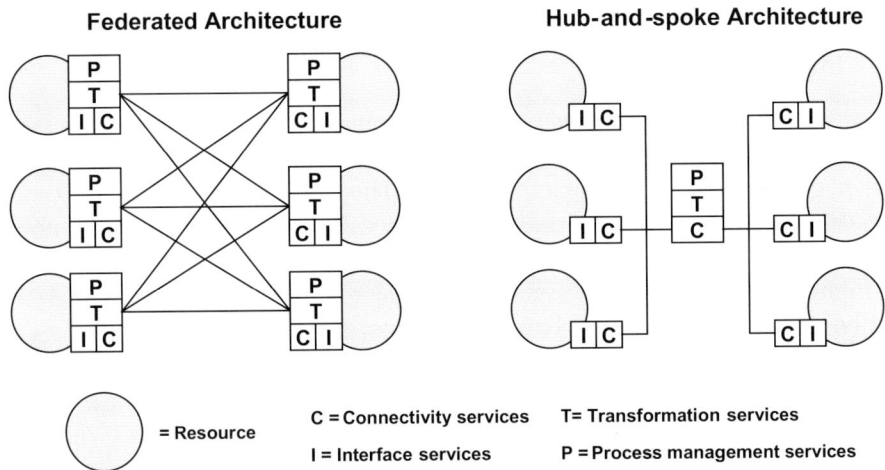

○ = Resource   C = Connectivity services   T = Transformation services
I = Interface services   P = Process management services

Figure 10: Two basic forms of IOS architectures (source Puschmann and Alt, 2001)

The general framework of Puschmann and Alt can be used to examine technical properties of the Vos Hub developed based on Informore's generic product architecture:

Data integration - The Hub architecture is a variant of hub-and-spoke. Interface translation services are custom built for parties. The, often proprietary formats are translated into an Informore specific internal XML format. Addressing and connectivity is very basic, using the internet file transfer protocol (FTP). The Hub simply places outgoing messages into a directory accessible by FTP to the destination party. Ingoing messages to the hub are also FTP-ed to the Informore server. The Hub does not send out requests, but passively waits for parties to send in orders and confirmations.

Object integration - As the volume and frequency of inward and outward messages are low (max. a few messages a day), the Hub does not incorporate any transaction management. It does not check if outgoing messages are fetched nor does it alert parties actively to provide inward messages.

Process integration - At this level the Hub offers some process modelling services. The route for each container can be planned. Timing constraints can be set on maximum allowed time leg between planned and actual arrival of a container. These are mainly business rules that can be built in. When confirmations are lacking, the Hub will display alerts on its web-based user interface. However, it does not push messages, nor emails to the parties that should act based on the broken business rule. According to Informore, its technically simple to built in such functionality, but it should be supported by parties connected to the hub.

5. Implementation issues

Few studies have reported on implementation issues and processes concerning IOS. Golden and Powell (1999) report on risks that have to be managed during IOS implementation. They have indications in their research that flexibility is unequally shared between initiators and non-initiators of an IOS. This has two reasons. Firstly, the initiator has a better coupling with his internal systems, by that the IOS increases its internal efficiency and non-initiators have not (in most cases). This initiator realizes a higher degree of internal efficiency, because this goal was to implement such a system. Secondly, suppliers are pressured to respond faster for the same prices and the IOS gives them the opportunity to keep in business (Webster, 1995).

We have not yet found a comprehensive methodology that deals with the risks and issues of IOS implementation. Within the Virtuele Haven project (Raalte et al, 2002), several guidelines are identified. A number of these are of particular interest to the Vos Hub:

1. create bearing, trust and volume between the parties linked to the platform, adding more functionality once trust has been built and users are familiar with the system.

2. work with open calculations to enable the various actors to accept the ASP investment costs, maintenance costs and running transactions costs.

3. have the ASP work with a SLA per application to specify obligations and liabilities for all contracting parties a/o. specifying ownership of data and data sharing rules.

These three guidelines can be used to get insight into how the Vos Hub is implemented:

Ad 1) bearing, trust and volume

The initial decision by the chain director to trial the Hub was not resisted by the larger parties since they regarded themselves as sub-contractors who were keen to establish further electronic integration with their customer. The Hub project has many participating organisations. The level of IT knowledge ranges from no use of computers to EDI connections. In the initial phase Overbeek (Trucking) asked for a computer, as they didn't have an appropriate PC to connect to the Hub. According to Peeman, 'ICT still is in its infancy, especially to companies like us (Trucking). Sure, the larger corporations, especially if they do distribution and warehousing, have it working, but the pure transport companies, that's real disappointing.'

In the hub project, Informore follows an approach based on iterative implementation of the Hub. Only bi-lateral meetings have been organized, no attempt has been made to create consensus among all chain parties through workshops or seminars. The hub's browser based user-interface has proven an important tool to demo and prototype the hub, but parties have not always understood that integration through messaging and creating adapters is essential for efficient operation. Similarly to all supply chain integration platforms, the benefits only come after all major parties have connected, but some of these wait till enough volume is reached. This may leads to an impasse.

Ad 2) open calculations

While the potential is great, there are also signs of wavering commitment, and misalignment of goals between the parties. First of all the parties involved had to be convinced to create linkage with the Hub. According to IT manager F. Scholte from Vos, 'The beginning was rather tough, especially to speak to different parties, to convince them of the possible advantages. The way of thinking in the supply chain together, to arrange this project, that was the difficult part, and it took a long time'.

The fact that previously private information has to be shared gave some difficulties. First of all the resistance has to be reduced and the organizations have to convinced of the advantages for them. Operational director J. Peeman sees potential when private information is shared, for instance to reduce empty kilometres. As his example tells, 'Vos has P&O as a customer and now an empty container goes north by train. Vos loads it in Groningen en the container goes to Veendam, where it will go on a train. But as Peeman is in Leeuwarden for a rush order for P&O, why shouldn't we look in the Vos planning to look what he has to do the next day?'

The participants have not yet agreed upon a method to identify benefits and to distribute the costs of the ASP (Informore) over the supply chain parties. The limited insight into the information processes and the potential of the Hub at the start of the project resulted in a start of the project without a quantified 'return on investment' calculation. The supply chain parties currently have difficulties deciding upon cost distribution, and possibly an extension of this research will be defined to devise a method to resolve this.

Ad 3) Service level agreements
No formal SLA's are yet in place. Although participants see advantages to share information, there is also fear to throw the doors open. This fear can be reduced through the independent ASP. According to F. Scholte from Vos, 'I think some people like to see this development, but other people are really afraid of this kind of information sharing, or showing information to other parties. But you have to from the beginning, you will be able to say if that is allowed or not, you are the one who will decide it, and together we will decide it. That is also I think the advantage of the hub, because that is not our hub, it is independent, so I think it is an advantage. If we came up with our own solution, then maybe we would have more difficulty in implementation.'

6.   Reflections and Conclusions

6.1. The Hub: Community or market?

Comprehensive surveys of ICT projects in the Rotterdam port community have been documented elsewhere (van Balen, 1999) and (Veldhorst, 2001). The port of Rotterdam is not just a cluster of organizations in the classical sense, but is a node in a complicated network of organizations that are involved in horizontal and vertical integration. An example of such a structure in the automotive industry is given in (Howard et al., 2002). Port community projects need to placed within the context of international supply chain co-ordination and info-sharing (e.g. pre-information from country of origin). It is also affected by international developments and the formation of consortia like GT Nexus. Some parties place their faith in construction of a common ICT system that serves the entire port community, possibly through a common messaging standard (Raalte, 2001). Other companies have began to experiment with private information hubs. The Hub as discussed in this chapter is particularly suitable for vertical integration of a number of companies in a specific transport chain. In fact, we believe one of the successes of the Hub is its focus on inter-connectivity, translating between file and message formats without well established standards in advance. Adoption of private information hubs through small incremental changes may be more successful than the grand solutions.

The Hub can also be compared to e-markets that focus on horizontal integration (alliances). An E-market like Transwide focuses on connecting additional parties but lacks the richness of private information hubs. As an additional party has a sizeable potential to the benefit participants (Garcia & Lambert, 2002, pp. 10), it is important to add more parties to the system. As Vos uses several terminals in the Rotterdam harbour and a few shipping lines, those could be integrated. After the first phases only one terminal and one shipping line are integrated. This means that just the Rail terminal Veendam – Rail terminal Rotterdam route is fully covered by the Hub after the full rollout. Further transport from the Rail terminal in Rotterdam to a container terminal supported by the Hub is limited to the ECT terminals and the P&O shipping line after the full rollout. When other terminals and shipping lines are added administrative effort can be reduced, especially for the road operations in Rotterdam and the planning department of Vos. The terminals and shipping lines could have savings as well. A barge operator could be included as well to give Vos the opportunity to choose between transportation modalities within its system.

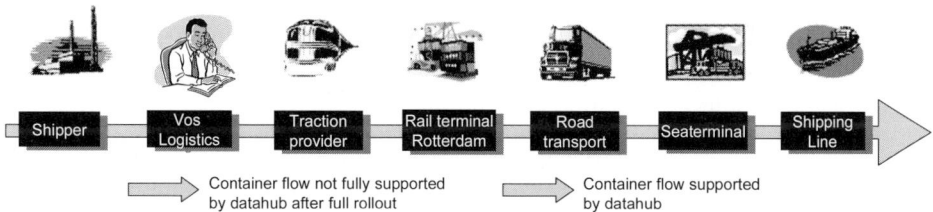

| Shipper | Vos Logistics | Traction provider | Rail terminal Rotterdam | Road transport | Seaterminal | Shipping Line |

Container flow not fully supported by datahub after full rollout

Container flow supported by datahub

Figure 11: Goods flow supported by the Hub after full rollout

Secondly, additional transporters could be added to create competition for the road operations in Rotterdam instead of long-term fixed contracts. However, Vosstated that they have no concrete plans to realise this in the future.

6.2. Information sharing and financing the hub

Information sharing within the supply chain creates network effects (Economides, 1996). While the effect of information sharing using new technologies is expected to increase with the number of parties sharing information in the community, there may be barriers to such a form of collaboration. This can be explained in terms of 1) the lack of economic incentives for creation of such a common resource in the first place, and 2) the difficulties in estimating the indirect spill-over effects in addition to the direct benefits of information sharing.

First, privately held information is by definition exclusive to the party withholding that information. That information is disclosed to other parties as required, often in a format that makes it costly for others to re-use that information for other purposes. While there may not necessarily be a charge for the information, the withholding party can exact a rent on others who rely on them to provide that information. The ability to charge a rent on private information makes it a valuable resource. Once private information is disclosed on the Hub, it has the characteristics of public good since it is both non-exclusive and non-depletable. Shared information is non-exclusive because multiple parties have access to the same information. Shared information is also non-depletable since using the information does not necessarily reduce its value to other parties. The air we breath for example is a non-exclusive and non-depletable public good. Assuming firms act mainly in their own self-interest, what are the incentives for sharing private information? When shared information becomes a public good, parties can benefit from use of the information, but there is little incentive for parties to transfer private information into public information. This is known as the free-rider problem, where parties gain from behaving in an opportunistic manner. Having such characteristics makes it difficult to create incentives for use of the common resource.

Second, the lack of quantifiable performance metrics within the chain makes it difficult to identify the direct benefits to individual parties and the indirect spillover effects on other parties. For example, party C may benefit indirectly through information sharing between parties A and B, even though party C does not participate. The difficulties in accounting for the cost and benefits has implications for the efficient pricing of the services. If all parties can benefit, they should jointly share the costs of operation after development costs have been subsidised. A lump-sum fee (or membership fees) is more justifiable compared to usage based (transaction-based) pricing in the absence of clear benefits. Asymmetric pricing whereby certain parties pay more than others represents a barrier to collaboration in this scenario rather than a facilitator.

Finally, the issue of ownership represents another barrier to information sharing in networks. Van Alstyne, Brynjolfsson and Madnick (1995) argue that: "owners have a greater vested interest in the success than non-owners" and "the concept of data ownership provides a mechanism for ensuring that key parties receive compensation for their efforts." Because it is not possible to draft complete contracts and satisfactory pricing arrangements in advance, the discussion on ownership can make a difference on the parties residual rights to control after the system is operational, hence providing them with the incentive to make the system a success. Some basic ownership models are discussed in the next section.

6.3. Ownership of the hub

In a study of 1802 e-markets (Laseter et al., 2000) define three basic ownership models. The first type are markets developed by independent entities or pure players. Most of these are dotcoms funded by venture capital. At the time of this study, over 92% of the surveyed E-markets were privately owned. As predicted in this 2000 study, since then many of these have disappeared. The second type are Emarkets founded by consortia. Various industry players, including competitors, join to create a common market. Famous examples include Transora in consumer goods and Covisint in automotive. The third type identified is the private E-market. These serve a single company to facilitate sales, design collaboration or supply chain management services among the trade partners of the founding company. Well known examples are Dell and Walmart stores. Consortia owned and privately owned markets accounted for 5% and 3% of the total in 2000, but it is expected that their share has grown since.

Laseter et al. outline a number of criteria that determine future success of consortia owned marketplaces. "First, they will need to create an integrated set of services that becomes the industry standard. Simply acting as an Application Service Provider (ASP) adds too little value. Second, a small set of founders must remain committed to the survival of the consortium and ensure the financing and usage fees that keep the e-marketplace afloat while it builds the desired capabilities".

In EDI messaging, the receiver pays for the cost of the message since the receiver presumably benefits from the information in the message. In the Hub, the pricing of transactions has yet to be determined. The logistics service provider charges per transaction, but to what extent each party should contribute to the transaction fee is still unclear. Identification of performance benefits and costs of information provision – benefits and costs of the Hub – can support the negotiation between parties on allocation of transaction fees.

6.4. Concluding Remarks

This chapter describes a case study of information sharing in a logistics chain in the Netherlands. We survey the architecture, the performance measures, implementation issues. We do not attempt to generalise from this case, nor do we suggest that the seven performance indicators in the previous section could serve as meaningful indicators of chain-wide performance improvements in other logistics chains. The performance indicators elaborate how parties in this specific logistics chain expect performance to improve through collaboration and information sharing.

Supply chain management, when planned, designed and executed effectively, is one of the keys to achieving high levels of operating performance. Monitoring the performance of the supply chain, facilitates collaboration and the adoption of a chain-wide orientation. Monitoring performance is not always economical, but hopefully, it has become more so with the use of information technology. One needs to keep in mind that information technology only serves as an enabler for further collaboration and information sharing; in the end it is the willingness of parties to collaborate, change their current ways of working and trust a new method of working before this can lead to success and a chain-wide adoption. Important to achieve such adoption is a clear insight in an (honest) division of costs and benefits.

7. Acknowledgements

The authors would like to thank Connekt for funding this research, and the participants of the Hub project at Informore, Europe Container Terminals BV, Rail Service Center, Vos Logistics, Peeman and others for their participation in the interviews. Information flows were based on an earlier Connekt report and modified based on the interviews. We would like to thank Thierry Verduijn, Hans Zuidema (Connekt), Willem Overbosch (Informore), and Frank Scholte (Vos) for their comments on an earlier versions of this chapter.

8. References

Alt, R./Klein,S. (1998), "Learning from failure: The myths and magic of electronic transportation markets", *Proceedings of HICSS 1998*, IEEE press.

Baalen, P. van/Oosterhout, M. van/Tan, Yao-Hua/Heck, E. van (2000), *Dynamics in setting up an EDI community, Experiences from the port of Rotterdam*, Eburon Publishers, Delft.

Barett, S./Konsynski, B (1982), "Inter Organization Information Sharing Systems", MIS Quarterly, pp. 93-105.

Brewer, P.C./Speh, Th.W. (2000), "Using the Balanced Scorecard to Measure Supply Chain Performance", Journal of Business Logistics, 21(1), pp. 75-93.

Clemons, E./Row, M. (1992), "Information Technology and Industrial Cooperation: The Changing Economics of Coordination and Ownership", Journal of Management Information Systems, Fall, pp. 9-28.

Conkins, G. (2001), "Measuring Costs across the Supply Chain", Cost Engineering, 43(10), pp. 25-31.

Culpan, R. (1993), *Multinational Strategic Alliances*, Howarth Press Inc., Binghampton, NY.

Davis, T. (1993), "Effective Supply Chain Management", Sloan Management Review, 34(3), pp. 35-46.

Economides, N. (1996), "The Economics of Networks", International Journal of Industrial Organization, October 1996.

Golden, W./Powell, Ph. (1999), "Exploring Inter-Organisational Systems and Flexibility in Ireland: a case of two value chains", International Journal of Agile Management Systems, Vol. 1, Issue 3.

Guglar, P./Dunning, J.H. (1993), "Technology Based Cross-Border Alliances", in: Culpan, R. (ed.), *Multinational Strategic Alliances*, Howarth Press Inc., Binghamton, NY.

Heijden H. van der/Wagenaar, R./Nunen, J. van/Bosch, F. van den (1995), "Redesigning Process Control Mechanisms using EDI: An Agency Theoretic Perspective", in: Sprague, R./Nunamaker, J. (eds.), *Proceedings of the 28th Annual Hawaii International Conference on System Sciences*, pp. 388-397.

Hong, I.B./Kim, Ch. (1998), "Toward A New Framework for Inter-organizational Systems:A Network Configuration Perspective", *Proceedings of HICSS 1998*, IEEE press.

Howard, M./Vidgen, R./Powell, Ph./Graves, A. (2002), "Are the hubs centers of things? E-procurement in the automaotive industry", in *Proceedings ECIS 2002*, Gdansk, Poland, pp. 1517-1526.

KMPG, (2000), *LDN Hub casebeschrijving*, KPMG study contributed to by Vos/Informore and funded by Connekt, 2000.

Konsynski, B.R. (1993), "Strategic Control in the Extended Enterprise", IBM Systems Journal, Vol. 32, No. 1, pp. 111-142.

Kumar, K./Dissel, H.G. van (1996), "Sustainable Collaboration: Managing Conflict and Co-operation in Interorganizational Systems", MIS Quarterly, 20(3) September, pp. 279-300.

Lambert D.M./Pohlen, T.L. (2001), "Supply Chain Metrics", The International Journal of Logistics Management, 12(1), pp. 1-19.

Lee, H.L./Whang, S. (2000), "Information Sharing in a Supply Chain", International Journal of Technology Management, Vol. 20, pp. 373-387.

Liebowitz, S. J./Margolis, S. E. (1994), "Network Externality: An Uncommon Tragegy", Journal of Economic Perspectives, 8(2), pp. 133-150.

Puschmann, T./Alt, R. (2001), "Enterprise Application Integration - The Case of the Robert Bosch Group", Proceedings of the 34th Hawaii International Conference on System Sciences – 2001.

van Raalte et al. (2002), Virtuele Haven Blueprint for a Virtual Port, Virtuele Haven consortium, www.virtuelehaven.nl.

Thomas, C., "E-markets 2000", case study, Stanford university EC-23, Graduate School of Business, available from http://www.gsb.stanford.edu/cebc/ cases.htm

Thompson, J. (1967), Organisations in action, McGraw Hill, New York.

Webster, J. (1995), "Networks of collaboration or Conflict? Electronic data interchange and power in the supply chain", Journal of Strategic Information Systems, Vol. 4, No. 1, pp. 31-42.

5.

Collaborative Planning Round a Fresh Fruit Terminal

Egbert Guis (TNO Inro)

Abstract

The trend of demand-driven distribution is visible in fruit chains, like in other industries, while traditionally fruit chains are supply driven. Also, the South African fruit industry has experienced some major changes due to deregulation and global competition. This lead to some challenging logistics issues, not only on the South African side but also in the receiving countries. The Fruitful project team analysed the whole fruit chain from South Africa to the Netherlands, raised relevant issues, identified potential areas for improvement and executed various pilots to investigate the feasibility of proposed solutions. This paper focuses on the pilot that was carried out on the Dutch side of the fruit chain to improve the collection of the goods from the terminal in the port by connecting existing information systems and creating transparency, making collaborative planning possible. The aim is to reduce the stay of trucks on the terminal from three hours on average to one hour and to reduce the phone calls per order from ten to one.

1. The Fruitful project

The South African fruit industry has experienced rough times since the deregulation in 1997. Since then the quality reputation of fruit from South Africa has been tarnished and prices have dropped. South Africa even lost price leadership over Chilean fruit [Broens, Tavasszy, Van Dyk, 2000]. Producers were ill prepared for operating in the new deregulated environment. They lost the advantages of the single-channel system, namely uniform quality and bargaining power. One of the main causes of the drop in price was the flooding of the European Union markets with second grade fruit of entrepreneurial growers and new exporters that found their own way to the overseas market. As a result, class 2 fruit has now been banned from export to Europe. Besides this, the South African fruit industry has to deal with global developments like overproduction and growing buying power especially the major international supermarket groups that gain more control and have high demand. These developments had also large impact on the logistics in the receiving ports. The predictability in the port of Rotterdam of the volume of fruit that has to be handled and the distribution over the fruit season dropped considerably and the destination of the pallets became more variable as well as the number of pallets per collection order.

Given all the developments and the current situation in the South African fruit market a working group of SANTF[1] took the initiative to conduct a pre-feasibility study on the cold fruit supply chain between South Africa and the Netherlands in 2000. The objective of the study was to identify promising opportunities for improvement of the supply chain for fruit from South Africa to the Netherlands. A number of opportunities were identified [Broens et al., 2000]. The most important need being the need for an integrated supply chain information system [Demkes et al., 2002]. The current information systems:

1. do not adhere to a set of specific logistics standards and guidelines that would facilitate communication between the components and/or systems;

2. were not developed with direct involvement of stakeholders in the cold fruit chain between South Africa and the Netherlands, and

3. focus neither on monitoring product quality and conditions nor on translation of logistic information that impacts on quality [Demkes et al., 2002].

These outcomes resulted in a large project named Fruitful. In this project several South African exporters, shipping lines, ports, an ICT supplier, the PPECB[2] and European ports and importers participated, together with SANTF, the Dutch Ministry of Agriculture, Nature Management and Fisheries, KLICT, ATO, CSIR and TNO Inro.

The aim of Fruitful is to make the whole supply chain of fresh fruit from the growers in South Africa to the consumers in the Netherlands more efficient and competitive. The way to achieve this goal is to create supply chain transparency for all involved parties by connecting their existing information systems and realising collaborative planning by using all relevant information available. The objective of Fruitful was to assess the potential benefits and costs of investments in an integrative supply chain information system that will overcome the problems. Three parallel supply chains were analysed and experiments with improvements are carried out to achieve this objective. One of the chains carries subtropical fruit (mango's and avocado's) in refrigerated containers and the other two chains ship pal-

---

[1]   SANTF = South African Netherlands Transport Forum.

[2]   PPECB = The Perishable Product Export Control Board in South Africa.

lets with grapes and citrus fruit. The difference between the two pallet-chains is that one of them is a completely controlled chain, still acting in the pre-deregulation structure and the other is an example of a newly formed post-deregulation chain. This paper will look in more detail at the outcome in one of these three chains, the new pallet-chain, and more particularly on the improvements on the Dutch leg of that chain.

2. Pilot Chain

Before describing the supply chain in section 2.2, the first section gives a short overview of the development of the South African market from the deregulation in 1997 till now. The last section summarises the actual logistics challenges.

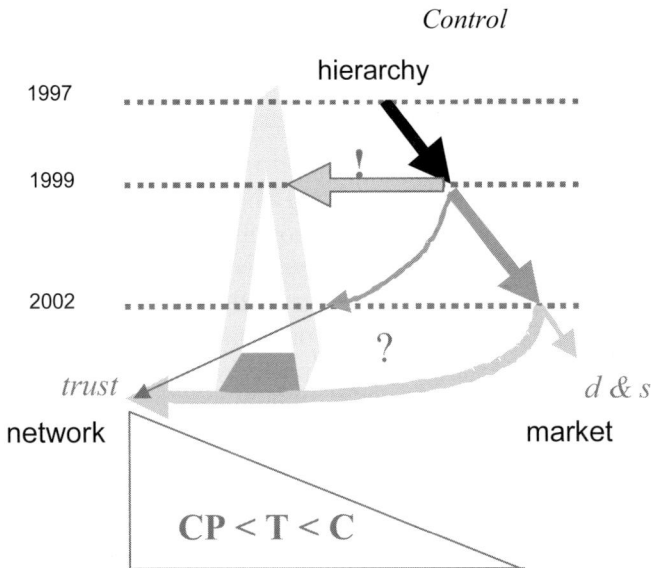

Figure 1: Collaboration model

2.1 Collaboration on the South African market

Collaboration can be distinguished into three different approaches, linked to each other as in a triangle [Hofstede, 2002]. The approach can be *hierarchical* with *control* as central theme or *market focused*, driven by *demand and supply* or *network oriented*, based on *trust*. This model is shown in Figure 1: Collaboration model. Moving on the axe from market towards network, connectivity (C) becomes possible, followed by achieving transparency (T) and bringing collaborative planning at arms length (CP).

Before 1997, the market was regulated and had a typical hierarchical structure, controlled by a few big parties. They used one ICT system for the whole sector, were transparent and worked together. After the deregulation many new parties came onto the market, trying to find their own way to the customers, moving towards a market approach. In 1999 at the start of the SANTF, the situation was chaotic and most of the parties wanted to return to a more structured situation. Many farmers were in debt. Quality level and prices dropped and the market share declined. Connectivity and transparency were lost. This was the feeding ground for the Fruitful project. In the last 3 years, the market found a new balance in being competitive. For the receiving Dutch market, the South African suppliers turned out to be an unreliable partner because it was no longer clear what could be delivered and produce that was promised went to an other market if it offered a better price. There is still a high demand for South African fruit in the Netherlands, so several importers tried to move upstream and make direct contacts with the producers or new exporters. The South African suppliers are still very 'market' minded, relying on matching demand and supply on global level, keeping information as long as possible to the chest. Knowledge is power. In this situation it is impossible to realise connectivity and transparency and take the benefits of supply chain co-ordination. Despite a competition strategy can be very successful, there are several threats in being competitive only. The retailers have increasing wishes about labelling and packaging, have increasing buying power and are taking control over upstream activities. The General Food Law is forcing traceability due to European legislation as of 2005. It is advisable to move from a market approach towards a network approach. *"An individual company no longer manages such influences on its own; competition changes from 'between companies' to 'between chains' and only competitive supply chains will survive"* [Christopher, 2001].

2.2. Supply chain

The pilot chain that we consider in detail in this paper is shown in Figure 2. Basically, each supply chain starts with the grower and ends with the consumer. If the grower and the consumer don't have a direct relation, these two parties need to be connected by a supply chain that should be as short as possible. All the actors and links in the supply chain should facilitate the flow of produce and finances between the grower and the consumer.

Unfortunately, the intermediate actors and links become more important than the parties on behalf whom they exist! It is a real challenge to let the farmers take all benefits of the appreciation of the consumers. The fruitful project team learned two things. Either the supply chain was managed so bad that the quality at the end of the chain was lost and that the price was not high enough to pay all the costs and leave to the farmer a margin related to the original high quality. Or the supply chain was managed so well that the margin was high but the money found lots of difficulties to find its way back to the farmer and only a small part of the money survived this journey.

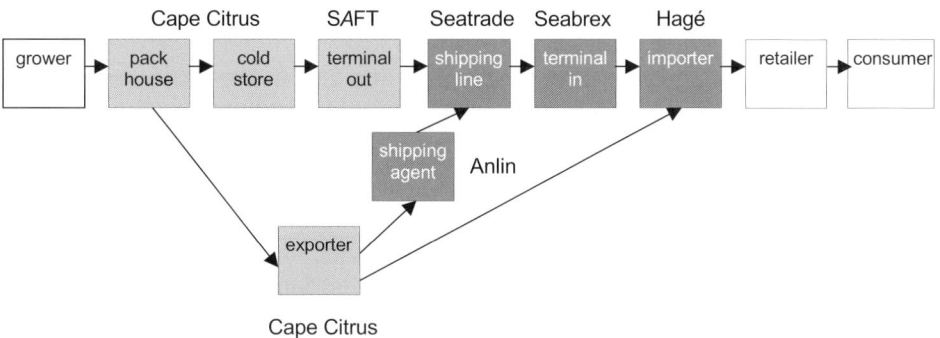

Figure 2: Pilot Chain

The citrus fruit is produced in the orchards of over 1800 growers in the Western Cape region of South Africa. The growers sell the fruit to one or more exporters. The best price is leading in making their choice for an exporter. The growers estimate the harvest in their orchards, starting six months in advance and updating frequently and deliver this information to the exporters. This information is very important because it is used to plan all further logistic activities. Due to the strong market approach and several other reasons, these estimates are very unreliable and cause a *fatal start* of planning the logistics activities. The fruitful project team analysed that there is no correlation between the estimates and the actual figures. When the vessel is in the port, it is a complete surprise what and how much produce can be loaded.

Cape Citrus is a relatively small exporter that buys the fruit from the growers. Cape Citrus owns also a pack house and a cold store. The growers harvest the fruit and bring it into the pack house. The pack house applies post harvest treatments, sorts and grades the fruit, packs the fruit in cartons and palletises the cartons. Each pallet becomes a unique barcode and the fruit specifications are captured in the Paltrack information system, linked to the unique barcode. The fruit is pre-cooled and stored in the cold store until it is transported to the terminal in the port. The exporter is the consignment agent for the grower, sells the fruit on the Dutch market (and lots of other countries all over the world) to importers and plans and co-ordinates the logistics activities, making use of pack houses, cold stores, depots, transportation companies, terminals and shipping lines.

SAFT[3] is responsible for the transhipment and loading of pallets to the vessel in the port of loading Cape Town. The pallets are scanned and all information is captured in the same Paltrack-system that provides a complete picture of the journey of the pallet from the pack house to the vessel.

Seatrade is an international shipping line and in the chain responsible for the transport of the fruit overseas to the port of destination. The exporters book the orders via Seatrades' shipping agent Anlin. During sailing the temperature in the vessel is checked regularly and this information is captured in the IT-system of Seatrade and Seatrade provides the estimated arrival time (ETA) of each vessel on their website.

Seabrex owns the fruit terminal in Rotterdam and is in the chain responsible for the unloading of the pallets of the vessel in the port of destination Rotterdam and the transhipment of the pallets to the storage location. On request of the importers and retailers they make the pallets available to transportation companies for the delivery to facilities of the importers or the retailers. Seabrex has the aim to move the emphasis from traditional stevedore activities towards the distribution activities. Seabrex positions itself in the market as a full service fresh fruit distribution centre, being able to fulfil increasing requirements of the retailers as the frequent delivery of small volumes and lots of varieties per order. One main trend is that importers leave the pallets on stock on the terminal and that the pallets or cartons are delivered directly to the supermarkets with higher frequency in smaller volumes and more varieties per order. To execute the three processes efficiently and meeting the increasing requirements of the customers, it is important to have timely all relevant information at their disposal to plan those activities. Although the vessel is sailing two weeks from Cape Town to Rotterdam, it was difficult to get all relevant data of the load on the vessel early and for that reason also not possible to inform the importers timely about the expected produce. Today, Seabrex receives from the port of loading (POL) a file that can be uploaded automatically in their

---

[3] SAFT = South African Fruit Terminal.

IT-system and from each exporter a separate file in different formats that also can be uploaded automatically in their IT-system. The POL-file doesn't provide the information about the destination of each pallet because the exporters don't want this information to be available in the Paltrack-system from competitive perspective. Seabrex combines the information of the port of loading and the exporters and delivers the results per fax to the importers.

Figure 3: Overview of Seabrex' fruit terminal in the port of Rotterdam with indicated the storage locations of the South African fruit

Hagé International is part of The Greenery and one of the biggest fruit importers in the Netherlands. In the chain is Hagé responsible for the arrangement of the transport of the pallets from the terminal in full truckload volumes mainly to their own storage facilities and sometimes to the retailer. That means that Hagé is not a representative of the customers that order more and more in small volumes with lots of varieties per order. Hagé receives the fax message with the pallets that are on their way to the terminal from Seabrex and capture the data in their IT-system. They send orders per fax message to Seabrex back to get the fruit delivered.

Finally, the retailers sell the fruit to the consumer. There are also a few other parties involved. The PPECB in South Africa and the Plantenziekte-kundige Dienst in the Netherlands do the quality checks in all relevant links in the chain. The goods on the terminal in Rotterdam are stored till the checks are done. These checks are not always carefully planned and makes the leadtime on the terminal unpredictable. The same is true for the Customs checks. That makes it difficult for Seabrex to plan the collection process efficiently.

2.3. Needs for optimisation

The current process on the Dutch side of the chain as described in the previous section, leaves major needs for optimisation. In the first phase of the project, the logistic chain was analysed in detail and a list of issues was raised that needed improvement, regarding the aim of the Fruitful project (Table 1). These issues were prioritised and the project team looked in more detail at the four most important issues. The fourth item on the list has to do with the last part of the chain, the collection of the goods from the terminal in the port of discharge and the distribution to the customers. It is difficult to plan activities for all parties due to lack of information, resulting in an inefficient process. Further analyses of the situation, the real issues to improve, the proposed solutions and results are described in the next chapter. The philosophy to optimise this situation was *'give to get more'*. Is it feasible to achieve better results by first giving away information, position, price, or something else that seems not to be logic to assist a chain partner realising better results giving him the ability to give something more valuable back?

On the South African side of the chain was looked into more detail at the first three topics on the list:

- the standardisation of codes that are used in the logistics process and information systems,

- the development of a standardised electronic booking module for shipping agent Anlin and

- the improvement of the electronic exchange of the mate's receipt from the port of loading to the port of destination and the back delivery of an updated version with the outturn data, including the results of the quality checks.

Although these topics, the proposed solutions and the results are very interesting also to elaborate on, they are out of the scope of this paper that focuses on collaborative planning.

Measures to be taken by		Requirement
Pack house	1.	Accurate information on carton (variety, grower, etc.)
	2.	Accurate, electronic data capturing at pack house
	3.	Standard codes to identify variety, pack, count, brand, target market, etc. for fruit specification
	4.	Unique pallet ID
	5.	Quality info and product history connected to ID
	6.	More accurate harvest estimate (volume and week)
Cold store	7.	Notify terminal of expected arrival time of truck
Transport operator	8.	Notify terminal (by phone) if truck will not arrive during allocated time slot
Cape Citrus	9.	Easy, reliable method of communication with exporters needed (accurate information on what product is available when, notification of changes in plan a.s.a.p.)
	10.	Fewer last minute changes to shipping bookings (volume, temperature regime, etc) as this causes replanning (Discourage last minute changes.)
	11.	Quality of fruit at start of voyage
	12.	Weekly bulletin (production, planning, quality, harvest, weather, diseases, etc.)
SAFT	13.	Indicate receiving client on mate's receipt per pallet ID to assist document preparation and avoid clients receiving wrong pallets
	14.	Damage and quality problems notification
	15.	Real time information on progress with vessel loading
	16.	Electronic exchange of documents
Anlin/ Seatrade	17.	More temperature regimes on vessels (e.g. 3.5°C, 7.5°C and 10°C)
	18.	Electronic orderbooking by exporters on website Seatrade
Seabrex	19.	Outturn report available sooner and by pallet ID
	20.	Damage and quality problems notification on arrival in Rotterdam
	21.	Feedback on result of phytosanitary (PD) inspection
	22.	Optimised collection planning (from terminal to retailer)

Hagé	23.	Quality report
PPECB	24.	Offer quality assurance and monitoring
Paltrack/IS	25.	Database with file formats of receiving ports for mate's receipt
General	26.	Create awareness amongst exporters of temperature regimes so more regimes will be available on vessel
	27.	Electronic information exchange between all partners (including better compatibility of systems)
	28.	Faster information exchange along complete chain
	29.	Electronic documents (customs) to simplify the process
	30.	Transparency about fruit produced and on vessel
	31.	Worldwide standard fruit specification codes
	32.	Worldwide unique pallet ID

I.   Standardise the codes that are used in the logistics process and information systems
II. Develop a standardised electronic booking module for shipping agent Anlin to be used by all their exporters
III. Improve the electronic exchange of the mate's receipt from the port of loading to the port of destination and the back delivery of an updated version with the outturn data, including the results the quality checks.
IV. Optimise the collection process of goods in the port of destination by connecting the information systems making the supply chain transparent, creating the right conditions to use all available relevant information and plan collaborative.

Table 1: List of issues that needs improvement

3. Optimising the Collection process

3.1. Detailed process analysis

To understand the situation in the Dutch leg of the supply chain, we need to start again shortly in South Africa. In this pilot pallets with citrus fruit from various growers and exporters are booked via agent Anlin on one of the vessels of Seatrade. The pallets are loaded onto the vessels in the port of Cape Town (or one of the other South African ports, Durban or Port Elizabeth, or the port of Maputo in Mozambique). A few days after sailing SAFT sends a port-of-loading-report (POL, which is known in South Africa as the mate's receipt) via e-mail to Seabrex, the unloading terminal in Rotterdam, the port of discharge (POD), and uploaded into the Caswell-system of Seabrex. An interface was built to translate the not so user-friendly print file format of the POL file into the Caswell structure. The POL-file gives detailed information on the shipped goods (Figure 4). This information is derived from the Paltrack-system, the current IT-system in South Africa that captures 90% of the pallet data from the cold store to the load terminal, based on a unique '3-of-9'[4] digits pallet-id[5].

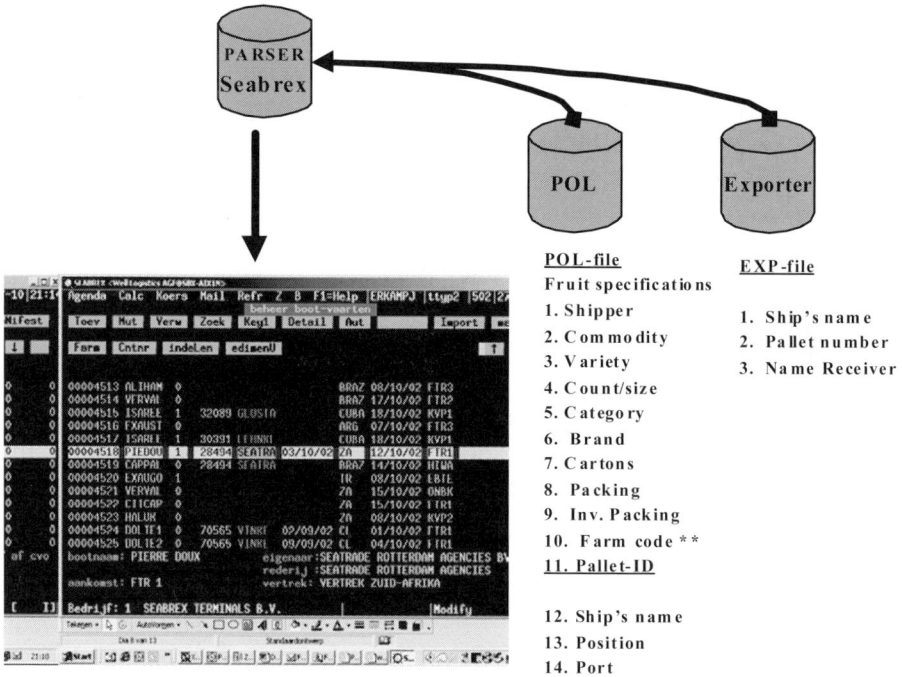

POL-file
Fruit specifications
1. Shipper
2. Commodity
3. Variety
4. Count/size
5. Category
6. Brand
7. Cartons
8. Packing
9. Inv. Packing
10. Farm code **
11. Pallet-ID

12. Ship's name
13. Position
14. Port

EXP-file
1. Ship's name
2. Pallet number
3. Name Receiver

Figure 4: POL- and EXP-file via parser into Caswell

Soft citrus is usually shipped in containers. If the pallets are loaded into a container in the port, the pallet-ids are captured in the Paltrack-system. However, if the pallets are loaded into a container at a cold store that does not use the Paltrack-system, the pallet-ids are not captured in the Paltrack-system. The pallet-ids are therefore not available in the POL-file as the container is sealed at the cold store and shipped door-to-door. In this case the

---

4   Term used in South Africa, it means 3 groups of 3 digits, for example 159 747 941
5   Within the Fruitful-project, Paltrack developed a secure website with customer-made reports that can easily be downloaded in the right format (excel for example). This feature was tested in item 3 ("Mate's Receipt/Outturn Report") of the pilot plan of this pilot chain.

exporter should send the pallet-id file to Seabrex, but this does not always happen.

Three to five days before arrival of the vessel, the various exporters each sends an EXP-file with additional information about the destination of each pallet (Figure 4) in excel-format via e-mail to Seabrex and to the importer. Seabrex uploads the file into their Caswell-system, combines the information with the POL file and informs Hagé (and the other importers) with an unloading list ("uitlossing") by fax message three days before arrival of the vessel[6]. Hagé captures these data manually into their own Baan-system[7]. Before sending this information, the Manifest or Bill of Lading must be received from Anlin. From this moment the importer knows his rolling stock and an unloading list can be made by the terminal.

The data of the POL- and EXP-file are very accurate. A few years ago the short and over landings were sometimes 20% or more, but now over 99,5% are correct. It makes no sense to ask for the EXP-file earlier because the destination can change while the goods are sailing and that happens frequently. Figure 5 summarises the various information flows.

Just before a pallet is offloaded, two barcode stickers containing the Seabrex pallet ID are put on each pallet. Just after offloading the Paltrack pallet-id and the Seabrex pallet-id are scanned. This means that there is a link between the two identifiers. From this moment on the Paltrack pallet-id is not used in the chain anymore, but via the link in the Caswell-system of Seabrex tracing is still possible. Each pallet is identified and the fruit specifications are checked. It happens that there are also name labels of importers or customers on the pallet. If such a pallet is redirected during the voyage to another customer, a confusing situation arises for the employee. Is the IT-system correct or the pallet label? After identification, the status of the pallets changes to 'I' (Identified) in the Seabrex internal system. When the pallets are transported to the place of storage the status change to 'T' (Transport). The pallets are then stored in the warehouse and checked by the Plantenziektekundige Dienst (PD). The status changes to 'O' (Opslag). Hagè requests Seabrex per fax to make out an order with client reference number,

---

[6]   It is technically possible to add the importer data in the pallet-id record in the Paltrack system and disclose them at a certain moment by the exporter so that they are also visible on the web-reports of Paltrack. However, the importer is not always known at the time of railing or fruit is sold while on the water.

[7]   It is valuable to investigate the possibility to realise an interface between the Caswell- and Baan-system to avoid manual data entry, therefore saving cost and improving accuracy.

which Seabrex then confirms by fax, specifying what is to be picked up. It is possible that the PD checks take place after this order has been made out. Orders are captured manually in both systems.

Hagé arranges with transportation companies to pick up the goods. Most of the time the goods are taken to Hagé's distribution centre. Orders are confirmed by fax to the transportation companies and to Seabrex, referring to the reference number of Hagé.

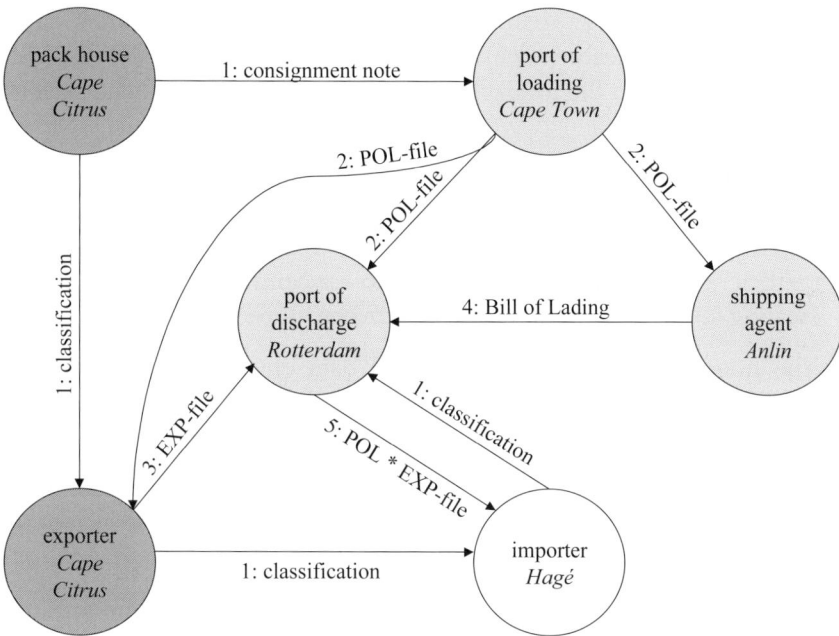

Figure 5: Information flows

3.2. Issues to be improved

Although it seems a straightforward process with all information available, there are several issues that are not satisfactory at the moment.

– Hagé (and other importers) only knows at a late stage in the process when the goods will arrive in the port and when they are available for collection. It is difficult to plan the collection. Trucks arrive (far) too early or (far) too late. It happens frequently that trucks arrive to collect an order that is still on the vessel and loaded on the bottom, or it is already offloaded but still in storage because the custom checks are not finished or the freight isn't paid. The truck has to wait or come back later. Truck drivers waste a lot of expensive time waiting and make the process more confusing by rescheduling their routes without notifying Seabrex and Hagé. On average the trucks stay three hours on the terminal where one hour should be sufficient and with 800 trucks driving around each day, they cause congestion both physical and administrative.

- Seabrex doesn't know when the goods will be collected. It is difficult to plan the loading equipment and employees. The first pallets of a new vessel are collected as soon as possible; the last ones sometimes stay for weeks. Because Seabrex doesn't know when the last pallets will leave, it is difficult to plan the available storage capacity for goods with different temperatures.

- Transportation companies, truck drivers, importers and the terminal make lots of phone calls – on average 10 per transportation order of which 9 are completely unnecessary. This result not only in high costs, inefficiency and preventing planners to concentrate on their job, but in creating an unpleasant atmosphere between all people involved.

- The huge amount of double manual data entry must be avoided. It causes only extra costs and inaccuracy. Seabrex sends a fax message to Hagé that is captured manually. Hagé prints an order and sends it as a fax message to Seabrex and transportation companies that are captured manually also.

In general, all information is available but not *transparent* to all parties involved, because systems are not sufficiently *connected*. This makes it impossible to use the information to *plan collaboratively* resulting in lots of time and money being wasted.

3.3. Proposed Solutions

The unsatisfying situation can be improved by *connecting* the information systems making the supply chain *transparent*, creating the right conditions to use all available relevant information and *plan collaborative*.

Seabrex makes already available on their website the expected time of arrivals of all the vessels coming to the terminal. As soon as Hagé knows from the exporter with which vessel the goods are sailing, they can look up the ETA of the vessel on the Seabrex website.

Seabrex is developing a secure website together with VirtEx (a Dutch ICT service provider) for customers and transportation companies, presenting the orders (reference number) that are 'expected' ('verwacht') and 'available' ('gereed'). An example of the website is shown in Figure 6. Via login codes it is regulated which orders a user is allowed to see.

An order is 'expected' after the identification of all pallets that belong to that order. Identification of the pallet takes place directly after unloading from the vessel. If all authorisation criteria are set on 'yes' in the internal system, then the order is set on 'available'. The authorisation criteria are the following:

√   Freight costs paid
√   Offloading costs paid
√   Phytosanitairy Certificate received
√   Bill of Lading received
√   Pallets checked and approved by PD

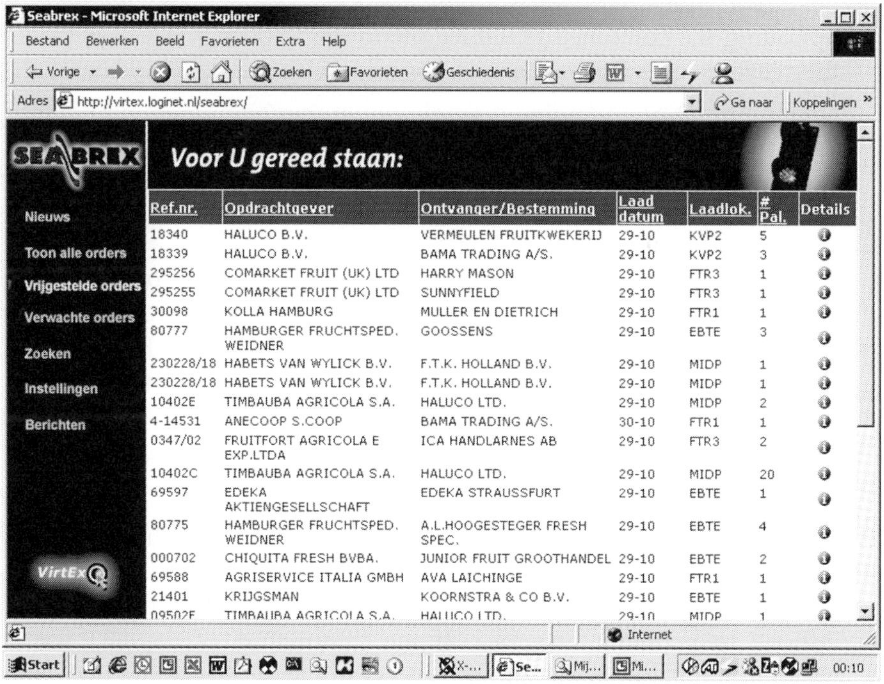

Figure 6: Example of the Seabrex website showing the orders with status 'available'

If any of these criteria is not approved, then the pallet will not become 'available'. The application can automatically generate an e-mail or SMS to inform the importer or transportation company if the status changes. The website also gives the order details and the deviations from the original order (for example different numbers or damages). The transportation company can see in which terminal the goods have to be loaded.

In addition to the basic functionality that is already developed by Seabrex, the Fruitful pilot team has supplementary wishes to make the solution complete, achieving collaborative planning by making the chain transparent via connected systems.

The proposals below distinguish between bigger importers like Hagé with an own IT-system that is used for the order administration and exchanges information only via EDI and importers that want to use the Seabrex website directly. The main information flows in the new situation are visualised in Figure 7.

1.   On the current Seabrex website, Hagé and other importers only see the goods they ordered for collection. It is useful for them to see also further upstream which volume is 'rolling stock'. That can be realised by uploading the combined POL-EXP-file to the website 3 to 5 days before the vessel is arriving in the port, together with the daily update of the ETA of the vessel.

2.   Importers (not Hagé) book their delivery orders on the Seabrex website, based on the available information, avoiding manual data entry at Seabrex.

3.   Hagé avoids manual data entry of the 'rolling stock' into their Baan-system if the combined POL-EXP file is also transferred from the Caswell-system via an Edifact message direct into the Baan-system. Based on this information, Hagé books delivery orders in their Baan-system and transfers them via the same Edifact-interface from their Baan-system to the Caswell-system, avoiding manual data-entry at Seabrex.

4.   The new Paltrack website, partly developed within the Fruitful project, made it easy to download the POL-file in excel-format that can be uploaded easily into the Caswell-system without using the complex, difficult to maintain, interface. If the information of the EXP-file is added to the Paltrack-system, the process of combining of the POL- and EXP-file in the Caswell-system can be skipped and the information can be downloaded directly by importers (not Hagé) in their own format at the moment that it is convenient for them.

5.   The current website shows only the status 'expected' and 'available'. The status 'rolling stock', meaning nearing the port, must be added and also

'on stock', which is the status of unloaded pallets until they are ordered by an importer for delivery. If they are ordered, the status changes into 'expected'. On the detailed information per order should also be visible the status of the five mentioned authorisation criteria, giving Hagé the possibility to estimate the remaining period 'expected'.

6. Hagé allocates the orders with the status 'available' to transportation companies in their Baan-system. Other importers get the possibility to download the orders with status 'available' from the website into a local VirtEx application to plan the optimal collection of the pallets and allocation to transportation companies. The loading date, timeframe and transportation company per order will be transferred for Hagé from the Baan-system to the Caswell-system via an Edifact-message and immediately transferred to website and for other importers directly uploaded to the website. An electronic message is generated for the transportation company. The status on the website is changed to 'allocated'.

7. The transportation companies have also the possibility to download the orders that are allocated to their company into a local VirtEx application to spread the orders optimal over the trucks. The truck registration number will be uploaded to the website as a result. On the website they find all the details of the order, even the quay and the number of the dock where to pick up the goods.

8. Seabrex gets a clear picture of the planned collections and is able to allocate people for loading the trucks in the most efficient way. Seabrex guarantees that a truck is checked in very quickly (documents already prepared and available on a self service desk) and handled within 30 minutes if the truck arrives on time. There is no longer administrative or logistics congestion. The status on the website changes into 'delivered'.

9. A proof of delivery is sent as an electronic message automatically to the receiver immediately after the change of the status of the order into 'delivered' in order to inform him that the pallets have been loaded onto the truck. The client has the possibility to download the details of the order with status 'delivered' in an excel-format, replacing the ASCI file with pallet numbers and fruit specifications that is currently sent to the client by mail/fax.

10. Stock reports and daily moves reports are available on request for importers and exporters to monitor their inventory.

11. Data will be available on the web one week after the status changed in 'delivered'.

12. Data will be saved for tracing of pallets if necessary and for statistical information. This information is only available for Seabrex and reports can be made for chain parties on request.

13. It would also be an improvement if the clearance certificates could be handled via the internet.

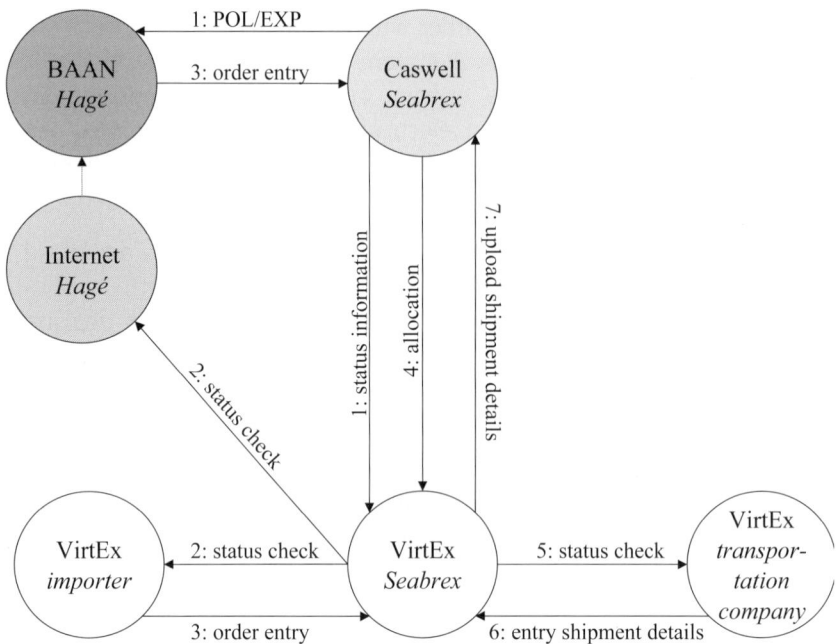

Figure 7: Main Information Flows of Proposal

3.4. Benefits

In general, each party has benefits from exchanging more information. Important is that it is a two-way exchange: "you deliver more and get more back". Also important is that the interests of the parties are not affected – each chain partner maintains its own role. A higher level of punctuality might be expected due to the moral commitment of exchanging detailed collection plans ("decent-for-decent"). With a clever system of rewards (VIP treatment, etc.) and penalties (low priority, etc.), most of the customers and transportation companies will stick to the rules in the longer term, thereby creating a much better atmosphere between all parties involved.

Each party has also more specific logistics and administration benefits, following below. Some the benefits are quantitative and can be calculated others are more qualitative and difficult to express in figures. The quantitative benefits are calculated on a high level as a results op this project. Table I summarises the roughly estimated best guess at the moment. These figures and those indicated below needs to be validated in the first step of the follow-up project.

Seabrex:

- Due to concrete collection plans the flow of trucks on the terminal site is much better: they go directly to the right terminal and will not stay on the terminal site for longer than one hour. Currently they drive too many kilometres on the site looking for the right place, stay for three hours on the site on average and sometimes leave without goods because they were not yet available.

- Due to concrete collection plans the allocation of people to the loading process can be planned much more efficiently, reducing the number of employees needed for loading. If the transportation companies guarantee the collection as suggested, it is also possible to prepare the loading process by transferring the pallets to the dock during idle time. Saving 8 man-years must be feasible.

- Significant savings are made on communication costs by avoiding the current irrelevant 9 out of 10 phone calls per order. With 800 trucks per day, 0,2 order per truck, I minute and 0,10 cent per phone call on average, a total of 24 man hours and • 144 is saved per day. The use of the current Seabrex website already shows a reduction in the number of phone calls. The planners are able to concentrate on the primary tasks: organising the activities on the terminal in the most efficient way. The savings need to be quantified.

- The information is more accurate due to electronic exchange of standardised formats. Manual data entry is avoided. If there are 160 orders per day, each of them taking 5 minutes for data entry, then Seabrex saves 13 man-hours, 1,5 full time equivalent (fte).

- It is important to note that the procedure must also be implemented for the "distribution customers". In that case the importer is not collecting the pallets in full truckloads, but the customer orders a transportation company to collect a few pallets that he bought from an importer.

– The implementation of the proposals for improvement gives Seabrex a competitive advantage in the market, gaining more revenues.

Hagé:

– It is known at an earlier stage what fruit is on its way to the market and the website makes it very clear when the pallets will be available for collection. This gives the possibility to plan the collection optimally.

– The potential saving on transportation costs is high if trucks arrive at the terminal for collection at a planned time, have no waiting time and do not return without pallets. With 800 trucks per day on the terminal site, all importers together save the costs of 1.600 hours per day!

– The potential saving on administration costs is high if data can be exchanged via Edifact with Seabrex, thereby avoiding manual data entry. Uploading data avoids generating and sending fax messages to Seabrex and transportation companies.

– Savings are made on communication costs by avoiding the current irrelevant 9 out of 10 phone calls per order. The 24 hours saving mentioned at Seabrex must be divided over all importers and transportation companies.

– An issue not touched at in the project but left unresolved for Hagé is the optimal structure of their incoming flow of goods. Instead of collecting all the fruit from the terminal and transporting it to their own warehouse facilities, they could also use the facilities and services of Seabrex. Regarding this issue, the project worked as an eye opener for Hagé, learning about the not completely known facilities and services of Seabrex and the way in which most of their competitors work or will work in future. Hage can reduce its transportation costs considerably.

Other importers:

– Hagé has one of the most structured collection processes of importers, because they bring most of the pallets in a regular flow of full truckloads to their own distribution centre. Most of the other importers on the other hand, sell the fruit to a retailer and the retailer orders a transportation company to collect small volumes. As the benefits will be bigger for these importers, it is important for Seabrex also get the so-called distribution orders in this structure to earn full benefits.

– Together they achieve significant savings on transportation costs and also on manual data entry and telecommunication.

Transportation Companies:

– A tight, guaranteed transportation plan gives the transportation company the opportunity to use the hours that are now wasted for other orders, thereby generating more revenues, together about 1.600 hours per day! They are able to charge a full service rate for these hours in stead of a much lower waiting-hour rate and they are often not allowed to charge all waiting-hours! The truck driver gets his picking order immediately, goes directly to the right dock, is sure that the pallets will available and does not have to wait.

– Savings are made on communication costs by avoiding the current irrelevant 9 out of 10 phone calls per order. The 24 hours saving mentioned at Seabrex must be divided over all importers and transportation companies. Fewer phone calls also means a saving in time for the transport planner and the possibility to spend this time on his core activity; namely developing efficient transportation plans.

Costs / Benefits	Seabrex	Hagé	Importers	Transportation Companies	VirtEx	Totaal
Investments	-50.000	-25.000			-15.000	-90.000
Transportation		25.000	800.000	-825.000		0
Manual data entry	40.000	30.000	215.000			285.000
Telecom costs	80.000	5.000	15.000	15.000		115.000
Process optimisation	240.000					240.000
Revenue	100.000			1.350.000		1.450.000
Fee	-10.000	-5.000	-30.000	-40.000	85.000	0
Totaal	400.000	30.000	1.000.000	500.000	70.000	**2.000.000**

Table 2: Roughly estimated costs and benefits

3.5. Costs

Table 2 summarises both the costs and benefits of the suggested improvements. The costs of realising all these system changes are about 80.000 – 90.000 Euro (roughly estimated). Hagé needs to adapt the Baan information system to receive the POL-/EXP-file via Edifact and to send the order information via Edifact. These costs are roughly estimated at 25.000 Euro. The costs of adjustments to the Caswell-system are estimated at 20.000 Euro. The costs to realise the requirements for the VirtEx-application are estimated at 15.000 – 20.000 Euro for the first step and the same amount is needed to make the system interactive. Besides this, the users of the VirtEx-application must pay a fee per transaction.

Half of the cost budget (45.000 Euro) is needed for realising the exchange of Edifact-messages between the Caswell-system of Seabrex and the Baan-system of Hagé. The benefits are primarily the avoidance of manual data entry and fax communication costs. The costs are equal to 1 man-year. Based on 5 minutes data entry time this is equal to 500 orders per week for all parties. There are also quality benefits in the form of improved accuracy.

Realising the VirtEx solution provides the biggest share of the logistics benefits. It avoids high telecommunication costs and improves the transport- and terminal planning. The costs are equal to a saving of 1800 truck driver hours at 25 Euro each.

4. Conclusions and recommendation

Connecting information systems and making information available to other chain parties give lots of opportunities. Giving more information away than usual brings more valuable information back then expected. The motto *"give to get more"* worked out positively among the chain partners. In the proposed solutions all parties are giving away data or even revenue first, getting back more finally in terms of lower costs or more valuable revenues. Creating transparency opens the door for collaborative planning with clear benefits.

Although this awareness was reached in the project, it took a long time to get there. All industry partners, not specific this Dutch leg of the chain, were passive project participants in the beginning. They were willing to have interviews and discuss the results of the research phase of the project, wre hesitant with respect to implementing changes in their own processes. Changing this attitude was difficult to achieve. The benefits of the first nine months of the project consisted mainly bringing all chain partners in direct contact with each other. It was striking that most of the operational managers never met each other before and only communicated by phone. Talking face-to-face and visiting each other's company created a higher notion of the "other side" of the processes. Long existing inefficiencies were solved in a few minutes! Chain partners talk most of the time only on commercial level, negotiating about the rates that have to go down each year with cents per unit. Setting operational managers together starts a negotiation about optimisation the process and lowering the costs with euros per unit. *"Pound wise, penny foolish"*. Bringing together the people was one of the most difficult parts of the project but turned out to be the most successful. After the first nine-month period, the progress described in this paper was realised in 3 months.

The costs for connecting large, traditional information systems are still high and the interfaces are specific and not flexible. The new generation Internet applications are open and easy to interface with other systems via common used formats. This opens opportunities for the future!

The costs of the system changes are high to realise the changes within the Fruitful project. It is strongly recommended to realise the proposed solutions in a follow up project to realise also the promising benefits.

5. References

TNO Inro, ATO, CSIR (2003), Fruitful D4: A vision on an innovative fruit chain, TNO Inro, Delft.

TNO Inro, ATO, CSIR (2003), Fruitful D2: Chain analysis and user requirements, TNO Inro, Delft.

TNO Inro, ATO, CSIR (2003), Fruitful D5: Pilot results, TNO Inro, Delft.

6.
Distributed Rotation Planning for Container Barges in the Port of Rotterdam

Marco Melis, Ian Miller (Initi8, Rotterdam)
Michael Kentrop, Bas van Eck, Mark Leenaarts (Illyan, Amsterdam)
Martijn Schut, Jan Treur (Free University Amsterdam)

Abstract

The transport of containers by barges has a share of approximately 40% of the containers transported from and to the hinterland of the Port of Rotterdam. The planning and coordination of the rotation of the barges in the port is still a complex task. Barge operators have to make reservations with on average eight different terminal operators. Due to delays and changes in the quantities of containers to be load and unloaded many changes have to made to the schedule during the execution of the rotation. The lack of transparency in the availability of terminal capacity creates inefficient rotations in the port and causes much frustration with each of the parties. To find a solution to these problems, the 'APPROACH consortium', comprising Free University Amsterdam, Illyan, Initi8 and the Rotterdam Municipal Harbour Service, explore the application of distributed planning supported by agent technology. This new technology has advantages over concepts that were suggested and based on centralized decision making and data collection.

1. The container barge handling problem in the port of Rotterdam

Rotterdam is a key container transhipment port in the northwest of Europe. The quality of a port's hinterland connections is becoming an increasingly decisive competitive factor. Until recently, road traffic was by far the primary hinterland connection. However, since the early 1980s, the Rhine has increasingly been recognised as a 'natural' connection with the German hinterland. Currently commanding a 40% market share, inland container shipping has in recent decades developed into a vital hinterland connection. Although barges are not a fast mode of transport, they can be operated according to regular shipping schedules. Their success can largely be attributed to the scale of operations and the ability to operate regular services. Inland shipping has become an inexpensive and reliable link in the logistics chain.

As a result of spectacular growth, container transhipment capacity in Rotterdam is now under pressure. Barges are handled at the terminal's quayside, using the same transhipment capacity (i.e. cranes and quays) as large seagoing vessels, placing ever greater demands on effective and reliable planning. In addition to the co-ordination of handling seagoing vessels and barges, there is another complicating factor affecting transhipment capacity planning: barges in the port of Rotterdam call at an average of eight terminals. The average rotation time is approximately 22.5 hours, of which only 7.5 hours are used for loading and unloading. The remaining time is spent sailing and waiting

To reduce the rotation time, barge operator aim to plan the visits to the various terminals as tight as possible. The complicated nature of this planning is borne out by the fact that only 62% of the barges leave the port of Rotterdam on time, taking into account a time margin of 60% (stichting RIL, 1998). This does not tally with the inland shipping's reputation as 'reliable and inexpensive'.

In this paper we describe the 'APPROACH' project. With the 'APPROACH' project, Initi8, together with the Rotterdam Municipal Port Authority has taken the initiative to investigate ways to improve the barge handling planning process in Rotterdam. The key question of the project is how to co-ordinate the various schedules and how to respond to schedule deviations. To find a solution to these problems, the 'APPROACH consortium', comprising Free University Amsterdam, Illyan, Initi8 and the Rotterdam Municipal Harbour Service, is investigating the application of distributed planning supported by agent technology. This new technology has advantages over concepts that were suggested and based on centralized decision making and data collection.

The outline of this paper is as follows. First, we describe the barge handling process, followed by the bottlenecks identified in the coordination and planning in the port. Section four describes the concepts and projects that have been initiated in the part five years to solve the problems. In section 5, the concept of distributed port rotation planning are presented. The projected steps of the application of agent technology in APPROACH are described in section 6.

2. The barge handling process

Barge operators are responsible for cargo handling and co-ordinating inland shipping activities. They operate the inland shuttles between the port and the hinterland and, in consultation with the captain, determine the order of calling at the various terminals. It is vital that capacity reservations are made well in advance, particularly when larger terminals are concerned. After all, barge operators want to achieve rapid and, more important, reliable barge handling.

Terminal operators are responsible for the transhipment of containers from seagoing vessels to other means of transport or hinterland transport. To facilitate the scheduling of the transhipment activities, they need to know well in advance how many containers are to be loaded / unloaded and at what time. Terminal operators want to maximise the use of the scheduled available transhipment capacity.

Accommodating seagoing vessels is a key priority in scheduling terminal activities. Barges are scheduled in after seagoing vessels, which is why barge operators must inform large terminals at least 24 hours in advance of the number of barges that will be calling and the activities required. The requests are collected and included in the terminal schedules. The barge operator receives a confirmation of the scheduled times. In the event of significant discrepancies between the requests and the actual schedule, further consultations may be held by telephone. Currently, only the barge operator works to harmonise the various terminal schedules. However, he has no say in the final schedules, which are determined unilaterally by the various terminal operators.

Barge captains calling at Rotterdam must observe the agreed schedule. However, the schedule may be disrupted for many reasons. A delay that arises at one terminal means that the barge will be late at the next terminal (domino effect). Captains and terminal operators often try to change the schedule to avoid unnecessary waiting and underutilisation of terminal capacity. However, as information about schedule deviations and available transhipment capacity is not always available on time or is incomplete, this is only possible to a limited extent. As a result, barge captains must often cope with long delays and terminal operators experience substantial underutilisation of capacity.

3. Bottleneck analysis

To obtain an accurate understanding of the problem described, the data from 'bargeplanning.nl' was analysed. This system registers barge operators' requests, terminal operators' schedules and data regarding actual barge handling [Stichting RIL, 2000]. It also records the key causes of serious schedule deviations. The data analysis revealed the most frequent causes:

– Delays during barge handling due in part to:
  ▪ lack of available transhipment capacity (cranes and staff)
  ▪ deviations in the number of containers scheduled to be loaded and unloaded (fewer than or more than were scheduled)
  ▪ problems with documentation, exemptions and loading / unloading lists
– Arrival delays due in part to:
  ▪ delays at previous terminals (domino effect)
  ▪ external factors such as equipment failure on board and the weather
– Unreliable schedules due to:
  ▪ unreliable estimates from barge operators regarding the number of containers to be loaded and unloaded
  ▪ lack of co-ordination between the various terminal schedules
  ▪ schedule 'slack' created intentionally by barge operators and terminal operators
  ▪ different deadlines applied by terminal operators for the submission of requests

Obviously, these factors are closely interrelated and influence each other a great deal. In order to address such a complex problem effectively, it is essential to understand the various causal relationships and their cumulative influence on the barge handling process. These relationships were assessed on the basis of information obtained during interviews and workshops with barge operators and terminal operators. Figure 1 depicts the causal relationships and feedback patterns in a system dynamic model of the barge planning and handling process.

At the heart of the model is the number of barges queuing at the terminal before being handled and leaving. Depending on the deadline for requests to visit a terminal, the terminal operator receives the requests from the barge operators one or several days in advance. Obviously, requests submitted a couple of days before the actual visit are not completely reliable since barge operators have not yet received all the bookings and must estimate the number of containers to be loaded and unloaded. Estimates made well in advance are even less reliable. The reliability of requests also depends on the extent to which barge operators include leeway ('slack time barge operator') on the basis of previous experiences at a specific terminal.

The terminal operators schedule the requests they receive and allocate terminal capacity accordingly. It is possible that they, too, build in slack time based on previous experiences of late arrivals and deviations from the scheduled number of moves. Calls at other terminals are not taken into account when terminal schedules are prepared.

It is therefore not surprising that, due to unreliable requests, intentional slack and lack of co-ordination, some rotation schedules are infeasible from the start. Against their better judgement, barge operators tend to stick to because in many cases the time windows for requesting visits at terminals have already past and some slack has been built in the in the shipping schedule already. Often, terminal operators are not even notified of potential delays that are foreseen by the barge operators.

As a result of unreliable planning, the arrival time of barges often deviates from the schedule. Unexpected delays at previous terminals and administrative problems cause further delays.

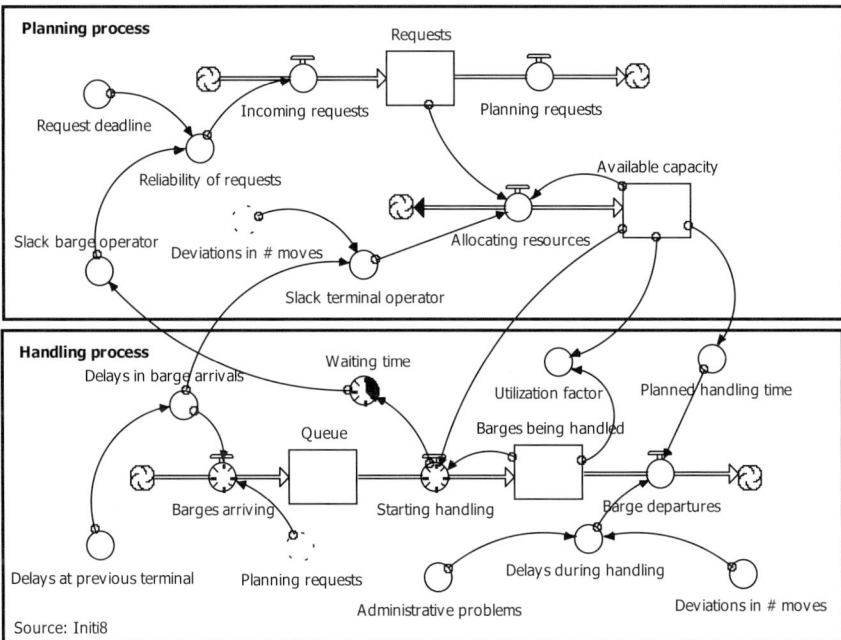

Figure 1: System dynamic model of the barge planning and handling process

In the end, such delays result in long and unreliable handling times, which affect barge operators in particular, and low utilisation rates resulting from unused terminal capacity, which is an important consideration for terminal operators.

Conclusions
Barge operators and terminal operators are both bound by a process involving increasing delays and underutilisation of terminal capacity. Each

tries to mitigate the negative effects caused by the other. However, the measures taken to that end may again create drawbacks for the other party, who will then apply additional measures, etc.

4. Addressing the problem

In recent years, various initiatives have been taken to address the bottlenecks described above. In order to clarify their link with the 'APPROACH' project, a brief description of the key initiatives is presented. In 1997, the Rotterdam Internal Logistics Foundation (RIL) conducted the B-RIL study, an exploratory study of the bottlenecks and the scope of the delays and deviations in the handling process. The study provided excellent insight into the complex problems and contributed a great deal to the conclusion of the covenant between the barge operators and ECT stevedore company. Some advanced solutions for transparency and planning were suggested, but not accepted by the participants. A first step to improvement was made in 2000. The Central Bureau for Rhine and Inland Shipping (CBRB) represented the barge operators in concluding a covenant with ECT, which included operational agreements regarding barge handling at ECT terminals. The covenant described agreements on handling procedures and performance levels. A next step towards transparency was the Barge Planning Support (BPS) project that was implemented within the framework of a European study. Its goal was to assess the feasibility and added value of stevedores' quay schedules that were published on the Internet. Barge operators appreciated the insight obtained in quay schedules. The stevedores, however, obtained no valuable additional information and regarded the technical solution that was chosen as being too labour-intensive. Next, the 'bargeplanning.nl' web application was developed to verify whether the parties observe the stipulations of the covenant. Its primary goal was to enable performance measurements during the barge handling process at ECT terminals. The system registers the planned and realised activities (number of containers planned and delivered, planned and realised arrival and processing times, etc.). The web application also helps barge operators and stevedores to observe the agreed planning procedures. Maersk Delta Terminal recently started using the application as well. Port Infolink BV (PIL) is currently developing Barge Infolink. This is intended to facilitate timely and reliable exchange of information between barge operators and terminal operators in order to prevent delays caused by missing shipping or customs documentation. Barge Infolink is restricted to the exchange of administrative information.

As is clear from the above descriptions, BRIL has been a useful tool for mapping out the problem. However, with the exception of the BPS project, no additional efforts were made to improve the planning process and harmonise terminal schedules. Only the planning process was formalised with the covenant and 'bargeplanning.nl'. As the list of initiatives and projects indicates, achieving improvement of the coordination between terminals and barge operators is a very long path with small steps. During the process it has become clear that none of the stevedore companies and barge operators is willing to give up autonomy to improve the planning and execution of the rotations in the port. The project APPROACH develops a solution for the barge handling process based on distributed planning and multi-agent technology. This approach takes into account the complex nature of the problem that is difficult to solve on a central level and meets the present culture and preferences in the way of working of the various actors in the port.

5. Distributed versus centralised planning

Centralised planning versus decentralised planning
To address the lack of co-ordination, it has been suggested in the past to develop a centralised planning system to register all container barges that call on terminals at the port of Rotterdam. However, such a centralised planning system raises some organisational and technical issues.

Organisational issues:

– The goal of centralised planning is to optimise the entire barge handling process at the port. The individual interests and autonomy of the parties involved are of secondary importance, which is unacceptable to the companies involved, who require full control over operational planning to execute their core tasks.

– There is no contractual relationship between stevedore companies and barge operators. Shipping agencies pay stevedores to tranship containers and conclude shipment contracts with barge operators. However, these agencies do not direct the operational process, which means that a shared view of optimisation is lacking. To make matters worse, the parties involved have conflicting business interests, i.e. a short stay of the barges versus a high utilisation rate of the quays and cranes.

Technical issues:

–   The barge handling planning process is a complex process and takes place within a continually changing and dynamic environment. Centralised systems, however, have rigid structures, which makes it difficult to respond to changes.

–   The logistics chain is a network that is hard to fit into the hierarchical structure required to operate a centralised system. Centralized planning systems aim to optimize the complete system, but defining a joint objective that meets the goals of all actors is almost impossible.

Given these issues associated with a centralised system, the possibilities offered by a decentralised solution were investigated. A decentralised system (or distributed system) is expected to simplify the planning process by dividing complex processes into less complex subtasks. Furthermore, a decentralised solution is better adapted to the network structure of the barge handling process and is modular by definition, which strongly enhances its flexibility. For these reasons, methods and techniques were sought to develop a decentralised or distributed planning system.

6. Multi-agent technology

What is a software agent?
'An agent is a standalone problem-solving software entity exhibiting the following characteristics: autonomy, social ability and responsiveness' (Wooldridge & Jennings, 1995). Accordingly, one can conclude that an agent is clearly more sophisticated than an object.

While Object Orientation (OO) focuses on modelling and rendering complex software manageable, Agent Orientation (AO) deals with describing and modelling parties and roles involved in a complex process at a higher level of abstraction.

An agent is capable of performing tasks independently (e.g. consulting a database, asking other agents questions, etc.) in order to achieve its objective (e.g. supporting a barge operator in drafting a rotation schedule). A system of several agents working together is referred to as a multi-agent system.

Agent technology shows its true worth in distributed, dynamic domains involving interaction between various parties that are not necessarily part of the same organisation, i.e., there is a loose connection between individuals, between organisations, or between both.

In analysing such processes as port container handling, a number of companies and organisations are identified, each with their own role and interests. Agent technology is ideally suited to do justice to this complexity and the wish of each of the parties involved to maintain control over their own business process. In modelling this process, each of the parties involved can be modelled as one or several software agents working together.

One of the advantages of agent technology is the rapid exchange of information between software agents in the processes of co-ordination, planning and collaboration that cannot be achieved by people by fax, e-mail or telephone. Moreover, since agent technology dovetails well with distributed processes, business processes need not be changed. Better still, they are used as starting points. A barge operator agent will be used to represent a barge operator, a terminal operator agent for a terminal operator, etc. Each of the parties involved maintains control over their own business processes and is able to safeguard critical business information.

In short: Agent technology is a natural way of supporting complex processes in dynamic, distributed domains. An agent is a software entity that can undertake tasks independently in order to achieve its objectives. The application of agent technology is extremely promising as it enables rapid communication between market parties, protection of critical information and utilisation of the existing organisational structure and, moreover, does not necessitate the modification of existing business processes.

Dynamic Organisation Modelling

The barge handling planning process is extremely complex due to its dynamic nature and the large number of parties involved. In collaboration with other research institutes, the Free University Amsterdam (VU) has developed a modelling method for dynamic organisations, which makes it possible to describe the behaviour of the parties involved and of the interrelationships. This modelling method is based on the 'Agent Group Role' model (Ferber & Gutknecht, 1998) and is designed specifically to analyse, design and simulate complex, decentralised dynamic organisational structures. The advantage of such a dynamic organisational modelling method is that it can deal with behavioural complexity, in particular for multi-agent systems with heterogeneous global behaviours.

In an AGR-model, an organization is described as a structure for activity and interaction of multiple agents through the definition of groups, roles and their relationships: an organization is regarded as a structural relationship between a collection of agents. Thus an organization is described solely on the basis of its structure, i.e. by the way groups and roles are arranged to form a whole, without being concerned with the agents that actually play these roles.

In APPROACH, the activity and interaction concerns the necessary communication lines between the different parties and the containers that move from barge to terminal to barge. Barges, barge operators and terminals are considered as groups that together form the overall organised multi-agent process.

Within an AGR-model, a role is the abstraction of a recurrent agent behaviour, linked to a status in a the organisation and interacting with other roles. The notion of role becomes independent of any particular agent, an agent playing several roles and a role being played by several agents if needed. The interactions define the relationship linking the roles to each other. A group structure is a set of roles and interactions between these providing a common (communication) context and rationale. The notion of group structure can capture goal-oriented organizations, points of view on a multi-agent system or design patterns in a software engineering perspective.

Needless to say, the port of Rotterdam is a very complex organisation. As mentioned, the parties involved have their individual goals; terminals benefit most from the effective use of their available space on their quays, barge operators are most helped when the barges make a fast as possible visit to the terminals. In this complex environment, some way must be found for individual goals to be satisfied as much as possible.

An AGR organisation model does not specify the behaviour of roles, of groups or of the overall organisation, nor how these dynamics relate to each other. To be able to analyse dynamics of an organisation at different levels of aggregation (i.e., roles, groups, and organisation as a whole), an extension is needed to the AGR-model. This dynamic extension has been developed in Jonker & Treur (2003), Ferber et al. (2003), Jonker et al. (2002), Jonker et al. (2001) as follows.

For further analysis a crucial issue here is how exactly structure is able to affect dynamics. An organisational AGR-structure is used as a basis to define dynamics (or organisational behaviour) at diferent levels of aggregation. Thus the AGR-method can be used to develop an organisational model that takes into account not only organisation structure, but also organisation behaviour (i.e., the internal dynamics at different aggregation levels) and its relation to organisation structure.

In terms of APPROACH, this means the following. The dynamics of a complex background as the Port of Rotterdam inherently thrives on its own structure. If this structure cannot support the complicated web of activities and interactions that take place, there is no solution which guarantees that any of the individuals achieve their set goals.

A dynamic organisational model then defines relations between different elements in an organisation (organisational structure), where the dynamics of these different elements can be characterised by sets of dynamic properties (organisational behaviour). As such, an organisational structure has the aim to keep the overall dynamics of the organisation manageable; therefore the structural relations between the different elements or aggregation levels within the organisational structure impose relationships or dependencies between their dynamics.

Finally, by applying the dynamic organisation modeling method to distributed rotation planning, we aim to lay out an infrastructure of the port of Rotterdam on which a multi-agent system can be built that may better achieve individual goals of all parties involved. The dynamic organisation modelling method supports the analysis and design of such an infrastructure and identifies the functionality of the multi-agent system to be built. In particular, the specifications of the dynamic properties of the different roles, serve as behavioural requirements for agents to be allocated to these roles. In this sense the dynamic organisation model is a high-level model, abstracting from the particular agents fulfilling the roles involved. An agent that is designed to be allocated to a given role has to fulfill as requirements the dynamic properties characterising the role's behaviour. Moreover, the way in which the dynamic organisation model is structured according to different aggregation levels, and the relationships between the dynamic properties for these levels, provide insight in how parts of the organisation contribute to the overall dynamic properties of the organisation. For example, if a desired property for the overall behaviour is not satisfied, by a diagnostic process it can be found out which part or element of the organisation is responsible for that (Jonker et al., 2002).

7. The application of agents in the 'APPROACH' project

The two key initial goals of the 'APPROACH' project were to understand the effects of distributed planning on the reliability of the barge handling process in docks and, secondly, to study the applicability of 'multi-agent technology' in modelling and developing a distributed planning system.

The 'APPROACH' project will demonstrate the effects of the distributed planning concept and the use of agent technology in a real time simulation environment, enabling the parties involved in the barge handling process to learn about the system and its pros and cons. The 'show case' that will be developed will also be used to inform other port sectors and educational institutions about distributed planning concepts and agent technology.

'APPROACH' uses agents to represent the parties ('barge operator' and 'terminal operator') and investigate and harmonise planning possibilities. The agents know the commissioning party's 'business rules', which means that they are aware of that party's priorities and planning rules and that they will take them into account. The agents gain experience over time and may develop some negotiation strategies and to identify the need for building less or more slack in the schedule.

The system consists of various autonomous agents. This requires a certain level of co-ordination, as they must bring their actions into line with those of others.

'APPROACH' creates an environment in which various agents communicate, receive orders from their owners – involving, for instance, the arrival and departure times of a barge at the port of Rotterdam and its loading schedule – and start working. Using the data made available to them, the agents determine at which terminals the barge should call and in what order. The next step is to ask the terminal operators about the available capacity and, subsequently, select the best options and present them to the commissioning party. If necessary, the agent of another barge operator can be approached to negotiate about a scheduled time slot. The selected time slots are registered in the APPROACH system.

An example of the interactive process between agents is provided below. Only one form of co-ordination is illustrated, namely the initial shipping schedule planned by a barge operator. Other forms of co-ordination as described above have been omitted for brevity's sake.

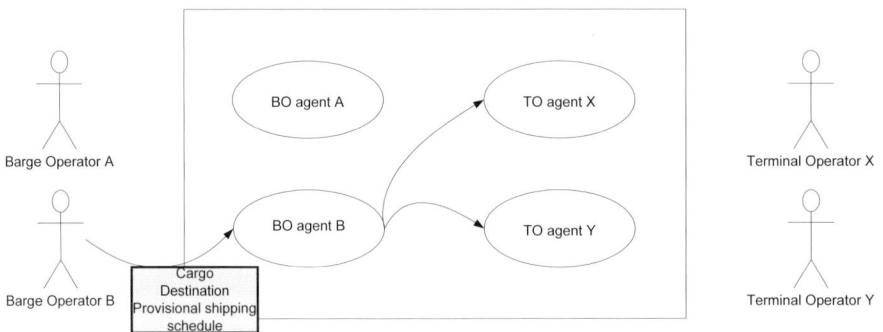

Figure 2: Through his agent, a barge operator registers his cargo, destination and provisional shipping schedule involving several terminals in the system

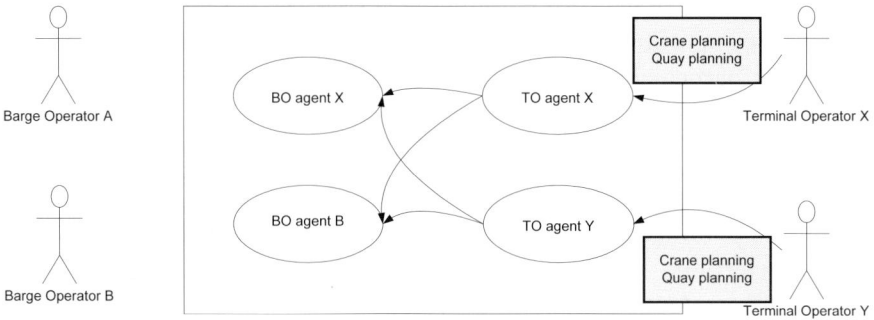

Figure 3: The various terminal operators' agents inform the barge operators' agents about the available time slots and capacity

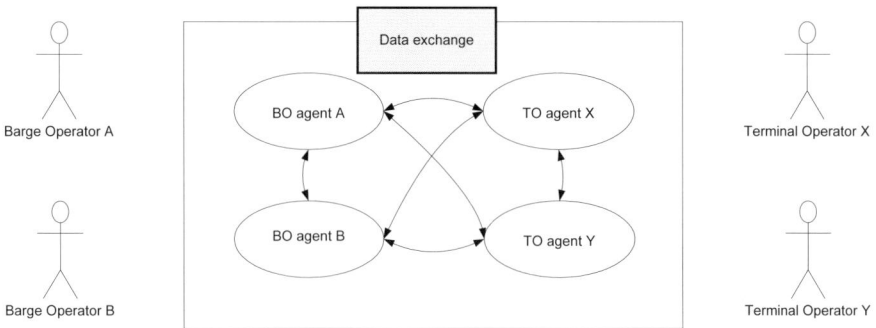

Figure 4: The agents negotiate on the basis of the information exchanged

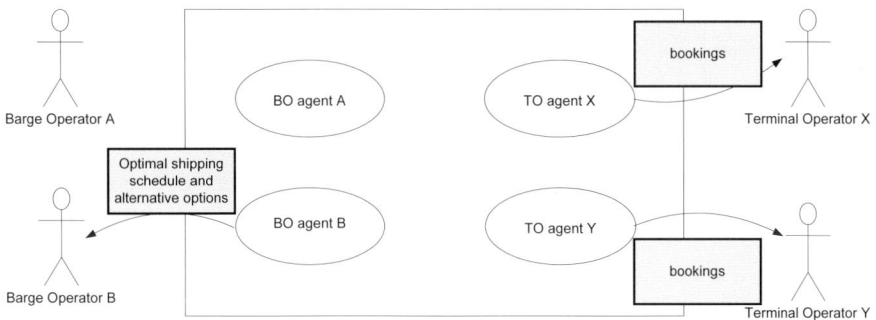

Figure 5: The agents report the options to the commissioning party

The bookings made with the terminal operators are not definite. Bookings and planning schedules should be confirmed by the commissioning parties themselves, particularly in phase I of 'APPROACH'.

Functionality
Functionality of the distributed planning system:

– Information exchange between parties, in which the information owner can determine which information is to be released to whom. For example, a terminal operator's quay schedule is released to barge operators, but not to other terminal operators.
– Co-ordinating and optimising planning between barge operators and terminal operators.
– Online generator of alternative, schedules following delays at a certain location.

The 'APPROACH' pilot will comprise the following elements:

– The Illyan multi-agent framework (agent communication, rule-based reasoning mechanism, agent environment, etc.)
– APPROACH platform (application-server, database, etc.)
– Quay planning (man-machine interface (MMI), data structure, database)
– business rule editor
– circulation generation
– circulation co-ordination (dynamic planning)

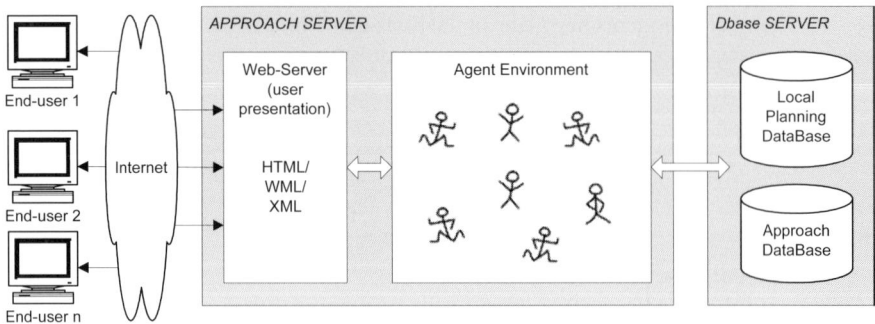

Figure 6: The global architecture of APPROACH

Development path
It is expected that a phased development path will be required to ensure successful implementation of the 'APPROACH' concept in the port of Rotterdam.

Phase 1 (completed): Problem analysis and a possible cost-benefit scenario for the decentralised planning system, in other words determining whether the scope of the problem is really that wide and whether the system will eventually be cost-effective.

Phase 2 (in execution): Technical feasibility assessment and development of a pilot application.

Phase 3: If there is sufficient support among the barge operators and terminal operators in the port, the best solution will be implemented in a pilot-environment. The functionality of APPROACH will primarily consist of supporting the preparation of rotation schedules. The labour intensive activity of gathering data and coordination will take place automatically with a number of options as the result. The barge planner will still select the most appropriate option and confirm this to the terminal.

Phase 4: As the system becomes more widely accepted, its functionality may be extended. More barge operators and terminal operators can access the system. Barge operators and terminal operators may negotiate to achieve further optimisation and deal with disruptions (barge operators negotiating about time slots)

8. References

Ferber, J./Gutknecht, O. (1998), "A meta-model for the analysis and design of organisations in multi-agent systems", in: *Proceedings of the Third International Conference on Multi-Agent Systems (ICMAS'98)*, IEEE Computer Society Press, pp. 128-135.

Ferber, J./Gutknecht, O./Jonker, C.M./Mueller, J.P./Treur, J. (2001), "Organization Models and Behavioural Requirements Specification for Multi-Agent Systems", in: Demazeau, Y./Garijo, F. (eds.), *Multi-Agent System Organisations.* Proceedings of MAAMAW'01, 2001. To be published by Kluwer, 2003.

Jonker, C.M./Treur, J., "Relating Structure and Dynamics in an Organisation Model", in: Sichman, J.S./Bousquet, F. /Davidson, P. (eds.), *Multi-Agent-Based Simulation,* Proceedings of the Third International Workshop on Multi-Agent Based Simulation, MABS'02. Lecture Notes in AI, Vol. 2581, Springer Verlag. In press, 2003.

Jonker, C.M./Letia, I.A./Treur, J. (2002), "Diagnosis of the Dynamics within an Organisation by Trace Checking of Behavioural Requirements", in: Wooldridge, M./Weiss, G./Ciancarini, P. (eds.), *Agent-Oriented Software Engineering II, Proc.*

AOSE'01. Lecture Notes in Computer Science, Vol. 2222, Springer Verlag, 2002, pp. 17-32.

Jonker, C.M./Treur, J./Wijngaards, W.C.A. (2001), "Temporal Languages for Simulation and Analysis of the Dynamics Within an Organisation", in: Dunin-Keplicz, B. /Nawarecki, E. (eds.), *From Theory to Practice in Multi-Agent Systems*, Proceedings of the Second International Workshop of Central and Eastern Europe on Multi-Agent Systems, CEEMAS'01, 2001. Lecture Notes in AI, Vol. 2296, Springer Verlag, 2002, pp. 151-160.

Stichting RIL, CBRB, TNO-Inro: B-RIL Werkdocument, Afhandeling Containerbinnenvaart Rotterdam, 1998.

Stichting RIL; Functioneel ontwerp Bargeplanning.nl, 2000

Wooldridge, M./Jennings, N.R., "Intelligent Agents: Theory and Practice", in: Knowledge Engineering Review, 10(2), 1995.

7.

Travail, Transparency and Trust:
A Case Study of Computer-Supported Collaborative
Supply Chain Planning in High-Tech Electronics[1]

Henk Akkermans (Eindhoven University of Technology/Minase B.V.)
Paul Bogerd (Minase B.V.), Jan van Doremalen (CQM B.V.)

Abstract

Describes a case study of supply chain collaboration facilitated by a decision support environment in a high-tech electronics supply chain with multiple independent companies. In a business process called collaborative planning, representatives from these companies jointly take decisions regarding production and shipments for a large part of their collective supply chain. Particular attention is given to the interactions between levels of partner trust and information transparency on the one hand, and resulting improvements in supply chain performance on the other. The importance of hard work in developing the work flows necessary to support this joint planning process in starting a virtuous cycle of steadily increasing levels of all these aspects of supply chain collaboration is stressed. A theoretical model of the interactions between these aspects is presented, based upon a review in the literature. This model is then explored in an analysis of the collaborative planning case. Contains conclusions and managerial recommendations.

1. Introduction

These days, competition no longer takes place between individual companies but between supply chains consisting of multiple, collaborating organisations (Christopher 1992, Fine 1998). The complexity of managing such decentralised supply chains is obvious. All publications in this area stress the importance of supply chain *transparency*, of sharing data regarding current order and production statuses as well as plans and forecasts with the various supply chain partners involved. If these data are not only shared between

---

[1] A full version of this case has been accepted for publication in the European Journal of Operational Research. Thanks to Sander de Leeuw for assisting in rewriting this article.

independent companies but some form of joint decision-making takes place one talks of collaborative forecasting or planning (Sherman 1998, Raghunathan 1999, Aviv 2001).

What has remained under-researched so far is *how this supply chain transparency is to be achieved in organisational terms, how it evolves over time.* Most research simply compares a situation of information sharing with one of none or limited sharing, without addressing the question of how one moves from limited information sharing to full transparency. This topic is especially relevant for an OR audience because, more and more, OR algorithms and decision support systems are used to aid decision-making in these contexts.

This is the topic of the current paper. We look specifically at how supply chain transparency is created in a collaborative planning setting in the high-tech electronics sector. This planning setting is supported by a DSS based upon algorithms derived from hierarchical planning concepts for multi-echelon inventory systems (e.g. Diks and De Kok 1998). We argue that here, transparency is not just the result of the algorithms and DSS employed, but, organisationally speaking, also the result of reinforcing dynamic interactions between *trust* levels between partners and the level of transparency that is in line with that trust level.

Moreover, we show that both are created over time by working together and surmounting difficulties jointly, i.e. by what we call *travail*. In the French sense of the word, this simply means "work", in English it is specifically associated with hardships, such as a woman undergoes during childbirth. The more supply chain partners work closely together, the more they will trust each other, and the more data they will dare to share. This will improve their performance level while working together, which further raises trust, etc. These dynamics are generated by a set of reinforcing feedback loops.

This paper is structured as follows. We develop our theoretical perspective on the basis of a literature review and introduce our research method in Section 2. Sections 3 and 4 describe our empirical base, which is a real-world case in a supply chain with four independent companies in high-tech electronics that we have observed and worked with over a period of two years. A collaborative planning *process* was designed and linked into the existing planning & execution processes, and *tooling* consisting of a decision support system and a data management environment was developed and linked into the existing IT infrastructure. Section 3 focuses on this design. We describe the phases in the implementation history and the decision support system in Section 4. In Section 5 we compare our research model with the case findings. We close off with managerial implications and conclusions in Section 7.

2. Literature review and research model

2.1 The importance of transparency for decision-making quality in SCM

The importance of information sharing for better decisions was first asserted by Forrester (1961), who showed that delays in passing on information lead to demand amplification in supply chains. Since then, this "Forrester effect" has been repeatedly described and analysed, and was re-introduced as the "bullwhip effect' by Lee et al. (1997). However, this recent research in the field of Operations Research/Management Science is not always very outspoken about the advantages of information sharing between supply chain partners. For instance, Cachon and Fisher (2000) found hardly any benefits for the supply chain as a whole. In other cases, there is no benefit for all parties involved, only for the suppliers. One possible explanation is that most of the analytical models employed in this research assume stationary demand, whereas it is obvious that it is timely information about auto correlated changes in demand, such as cyclical market movements, that is beneficial for supply chain performance (Sterman 2000). At any rate, Aviv (2001) is probably right when he writes in his recent *Management Science* article on collaborative forecasting that "this study comes at a time when various types of collaborative forecasting partnerships are being experimented within industry, and when the drivers for success or failure of such initiatives are not yet fully understood" (p. 1326).

2.2 The importance of trust for openness of communication and hence transparency

The field of organisation studies has written extensively on the topic of trust. Nevertheless, trust remains an elusive concept. One recent definition is that trust is to be seen as "the belief that the other party will act in the firm's best interest in circumstances where that other party could take advantage or act opportunistically to gain at the firm's expense" (McCutcheon and Stuart 2000, p. 291). These days, the importance of trust for effective interorganisational relations is well established both in economics and strategy (e.g. De Jong and Nooteboom 2000).

2.3 The importance of trust for absence of gaming and hence decision quality

Next to the general importance of information transparency there is a phenomenon specifically related to supply chain control. This is the phenomenon of game playing between buyer and seller in volatile markets. As Lee et al. (1997) have noted, the infamous bullwhip effect is, if not generated, then at least exacerbated by "shortage gaming". During a period of shortage, which frequently occurs in an industry upturn, buyers tend to order more than they really need from a supplier, because they anticipate that they will be getting less anyway. Since all buyers do so, this strongly inflates the incoming order level, which then generates further amplifications upstream. Since the suppliers know this is happening, they tend to downscale all incoming demand levels. The only way to prevent this amplification from happening is if the buyer can *trust* the supplier to interpret this order information correctly and if the supplier can *trust* the buyer to provide him with correct demand figures (Lee et al. 1997, Akkermans et al. 1999, Sterman 2000).

2.4 Interrelations between transparency and trust

As the preceding discussion of game-playing illustrates, there is an other side to the relation between trust and transparency: the impact that transparency can have on trust. Again, this topic has been well studied in the organisational literature. Most findings cluster around the conclusion that communication, transparancy and trust are positively related.

2.5 The importance of social exchange for transparency and trust

This still leaves us with the original question for this research: how are transparency and trust generated? Partners get used to each other, understand each other better, as they continue their social exchanges over time. De Jong and Nooteboom (2000) label this phenomenon as *habituation*: "it is repeated interaction which leads to the forming of habits and the institutionalisation of behaviour. Any human activity that is frequently repeated is subject to habituation, which frees the individual from having to make decisions and thus provides psychological relief". (De Jong and Nooteboom (2000, p. 222).

2.6   Research Model

In this section we synthesise the findings from the literature review in the preceding section into our research model of how trust and transparency are generated. Partly, this model is based upon earlier research by the first two authors (Akkermans et al. 1999). It is visualised in Figure 1 by way of causal loops (Sterman 2000).

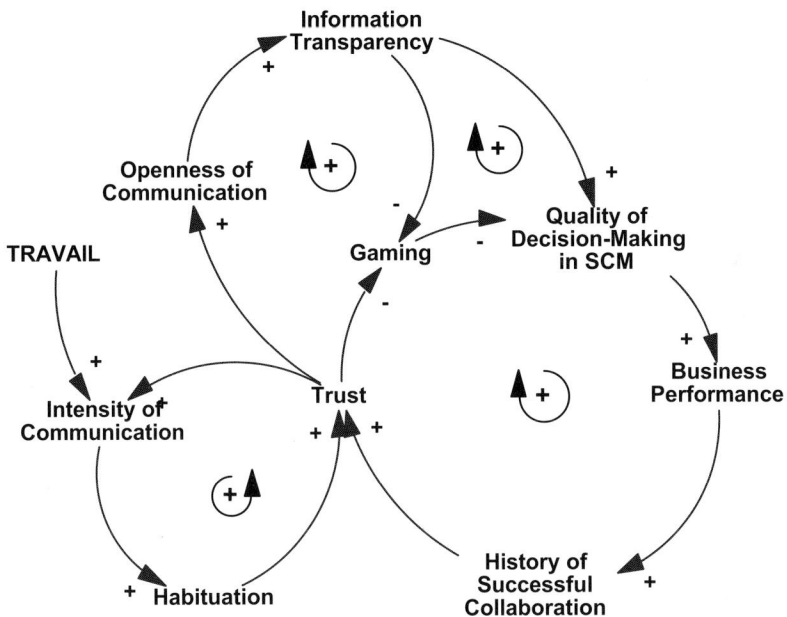

Figure 1: The theoretical model for this research

The model reads as follows: Supply chain transparency is the result of self-enforcing dynamic interactions between 'shared hard working or toiling' (travail), 'believe in the honesty, integrity, reliability, justice of the partners' (trust), and 'open sharing of all relevant information' (transparency). As such, it is the struggling on the long and winding path towards transparency that determines the level of success of the collaboration between supply chain partners, rather than its definition by management. A "+" next to an arrow indicates a positive relationship (and consequently a "-" a negative relationship).

It is important to note the *feedback loop* nature (Sterman 2000) of this causal model: increases in trust lead to increases in transparency, which improves decision-making quality, which leads to better supply chain performance. This then leads to habituation, which, in turn, increases trust further. The result of this is that partners in a supply chain often get caught in either a vicious or a virtuous cycle. If performance is low, trust and transparency remain low. If somehow this vicious cycle is broken and trust and transparency start going up, an upward spiral over steadily improving supply chain performance can be achieved. The "+" with an arrow around it indicates this reinforcing nature of a feedback loopIn the current research model, our interest is in how a virtuous cycle of supply chain collaboration can be started. Here we have found our notion of *travail* very enlightening. Triggered by the literature on social exchange and habituation as well as our experiences as action researchers in this case, we have noticed how trust and transparency grew gradually as the result of, simply, a lot of hard work by the people involved. It is the quiet accumulation of joint and positive experiences that has formed the foundation for the subsequent successes.

2.7 Case study selection

Our case concerns the implementation of a collaborative planning (CP) process, including DSS tooling, in the high-tech electronics industry. The partners involved were a manufacturer of integrated circuits (IC's), a number of contract manufacturers (CM's) assembling subassemblies and a producer of innovative personal computer parts. This supply chain was characterised by (a) a high dependency on a limited number of key IC's (10); (b) long stacked lead times (20 weeks); and (c) short product life cycles of end products and key components (6-12 months).

The primary objectives of implementing a CP process were an increase of market share through reduction of time-to-market, improving material availability and cost reduction through lowering overall stock levels and less obsolescence. Moreover, it was envisioned that collaboration at the operational goods flow level would contribute positively to collaboration in other areas (such as product design, supply chain design and capacity creation).

Our involvement spanned roughly 18 months and covered the design, development, implementation and execution of a CP process as a joint effort by the IC manufacturer and the PC part manufacturer. Apart from external and internal consultants, the project organisation consisted of logistic planners, account managers, purchase managers and supply chain managers.

3.   Case description: what has been implemented

3.1 What to tackle

When designing a collaborative planning process (CP process), a number of issues need to be tackled. Apart from the "culture / trust" aspect (extensively discussed throughout this paper), there are a number of 'hard' (as opposed to 'soft') issues to be addressed:

- The business case for Collaborative planning
- Definition of the CP process itself, including roles & responsibilities
- Links between the CP process with the other planning- and execution processes existing in the participating organizations
- Availability of appropriate data

Each of these topics is discussed below.

3.2 The business case for CP

Although making a detailed quantification of the benefits of CP is far from self evident, some calculations suffice to prove the immediate benefits of CP.

The (1st order) benefits will stem primarily from less *lost sales*, reduced *inventory levels* and less *obsolete stocks*. Key parameter in these calculations is the "reduction in information latency". ". For instance:

- By making a number of simplifying assumptions, it is possible to calculate 'lost sales' that occur when the upstream IC manufacturer is unaware of an unexpected upswing in the end user market (resulting in significant material shortages). When information throughput time is reduced from 6 to 2 weeks (which was indeed the case), these lost sales are reduced by approximately two-thirds.

- Likewise, it is possible to calculate obsolete stocks that could have been avoided when the upstream partner would have been aware of an unexpected market downturn (for instance because the life cycle of the product was shorter than expected). Again, reducing information latency from 6 to 2 weeks, will reduce these obsoletes by two-thirds.

Less obvious, but nonetheless relevant, are gains resulting from a more stable workload in the upstream production processes (due to reduced bull whip effects).

All in all, in this particular case, a rough cut –conversative- estimate of the annual cost reductions amounted to multiple millions of Euro's. The implication was that the pay back period for the project was expressed in 'months' rather than in 'years'. Seeing that the benefits case were so obviously positive, it was not deemed necessary to get to a detailed cost/benefit analysis.

Potentially even more important (but certainly more difficult to quantify) are the benefits of joint decision making, joint priority settings, sharing the 'information behind the figures', etcetera. Moving from a "fire fighting" mode towards a way of working centering around "pro-active issue identification & solving" an "opportunity spotting", may be the most effective contribution of CP. In our case, no attempt has been made to quantify these less tangible benefits, neither ex ante, nor ex post.

3.3 The CP-process

In essence, the CP process is a *decision making* process. Based on information representing the status of the (extended) supply chain, and on forecasted demand, decisions with respect to production and shipments are made in a *joint* process, for which a *joint* responsibility exists, and for whose consequences both parties are jointly liable. The decisions that are made in the semi-conductor supply chain are summarised in Figure 2.

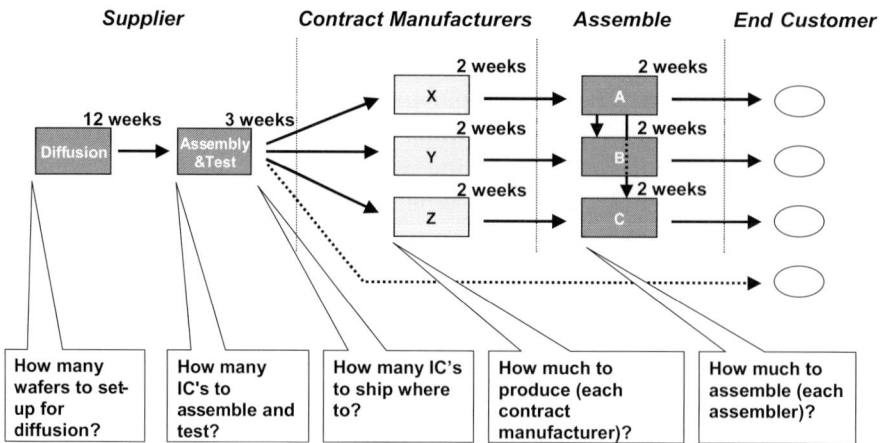

Figure 2: Decisions in the semiconductor supply chain

The dynamics of (the up-stream part of) the chain allows running this process on a weekly basis: each week, decisions are taken covering the operations during the next week. And in one go: each week the market situation in the (near) future is assessed, and evaluated for its consequences.

Where in many situations, a *monthly* evaluation of the market outlook is considered to be good enough, in this specific situation the dynamics in the market make a *weekly* evaluation useful.

The CP process consists of four sub processes (see Figure 3):

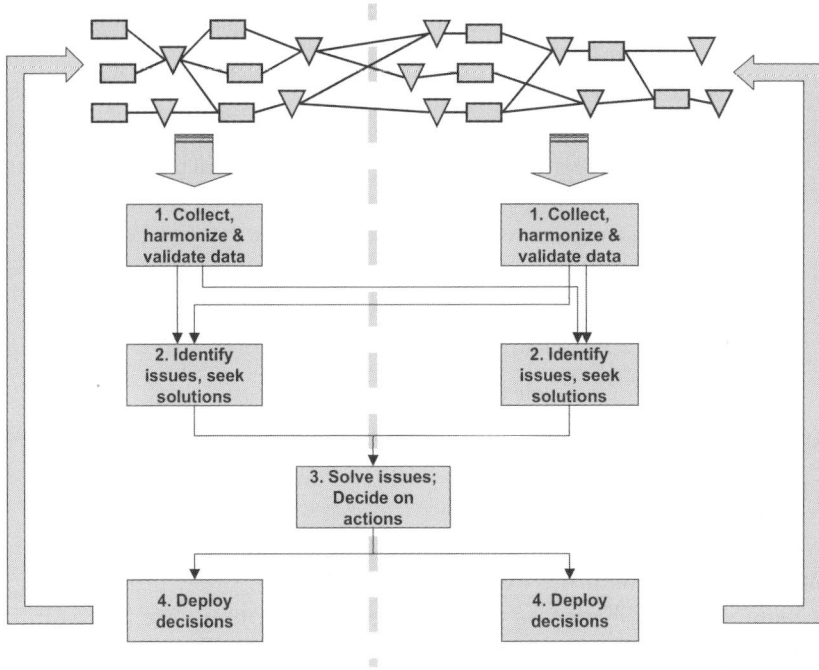

Figure 3: Four sub-processes in Collaborative Planning

1	Collect, harmonize & validate data
	Gathering (and harmonizing) from over 6 different organizational entities is an effort in itself. During the project, it was decided to go for a 'low tech' solution, implying that a significant amount of manual work was involved. On top of that: because sharing information implies 'opening up' for your trading partner, an additional step – aimed at improving the quality of the data – was considered to be essential.
2	Identify issues, seek solutions
	In this step, the new supply chain status figures are confronted with new demand figures. Potential issues are highlighted, and both organizations seek – internally – what measures could be taken to solve these issues

3	*Solve Issues, decide on actions*
	In this step, in a joint session, the 'information behind the figures' is exchanged, exceptions (e.g. a planned supply or demand that is lower then expected) are explained, and joint decisions with respect to next weeks' actions are made. Key here is that priorities in the up stream part of the supply chain are set consistent with the priorities in the down stream part. Also, establishing 'early warnings' on future issues (in some cases even 10 weeks in advance) significantly contributes to the overall success of CP
4	*Deploy decisions*
	Making decisions in a joint session is one, making sure that all players properly act in accordance to those decisions is another one. Here, making sure that the 'regular' planning and execution processes do not ignore (let alone override) the decisions is crucial, and far from trivial. For instance: how to avoid that the 'regular' MRP runs respect earlier commitments for starting production batches? How to ensure that committed supplies are not 'given away' to other customers?

Table 1: Explanation of Figure 3

3.4 Linking CP to other processes

Maybe the most difficult task in establishing the CP process, is to define a clear interface between the existing planning & execution processes on the one hand, an the CP process on the other hand. Among the things to take into account are:

– *Timing* → what is the most appropriate moment in time at which the required data can be made available? This does of course depend heavily on the rhythm in which the processes generating those data do run; finding a proper time slot may be far from trivial.

– *Deploying decisions* → In general, the *execution* of the decisions taken in the CP process, is controlled by the organizations' operational (ERP) systems. The implication is that, one way or the other, the output of the CP process is to be fed into the ERP systems. At the *transactional* level, this input might take the form of 'purchase orders', 'customer orders', 'production plans', etcetera. At the *plan* level, the input might be 'customer forecasts', blanket orders, etcetera. The standard logic contained in the operational systems should not override these decisions. At the same time, the decisions made during the CP process should lie within the bounds set by the constraints and business rules that are embedded in the operational systems.

–   *Redefining KPI's* → After implementing CP, KPI's may need to be redefined. For instance, -from an extended supply chain perspective- it may make sense to move inventory up or down the chain. The typical F&A department won't be too happy seeing inventory levels rising.

3.5 Availability of appropriate data

Data are to be provided once a week, and comprise, apart from the required master data:

–   Stock levels
–   Work in progress levels & planned production
–   In Transits
–   Forecasted demand

Surprisingly, the volume of the data needed in the CP process – as it is defined here – is fairly low. Since data are needed only once a week, and because the process covers only a limited number of items, collecting the data using a low tech (e.g. spreadsheet based) is perfectly feasible (though of course far from optimal).

3.6 The decision support system

Though people, and managers in particular, generally feel that decision making is a form of art and requires experience, intuition and creativity, it is also generally acknowledged that decision making processes are greatly enhanced by the application of appropriate scientific methods. However, decision makers will only use such scientific methods, if the supplier is able to provide an environment allowing for an effective stipulation of the ideas (easy generation of options at the required aggregation level) and a rapid analysis of those ideas (fast on-line generation of highly visible quantitative insights). This then has been the challenge that has been met in this case with the DSS environment that was developed.

The collaborative planning DSS environment aims at the co-ordination of material flows through a complex supply network with multiple independent players. This co-ordination makes sense only if it generates an improvement of the overall performance and decreases the total supply chain costs. To accomplish this, a tailored software environment has been put in place providing a means to define supply chain structures, supporting the gathering and preparation of relevant data from the multiple network entities, creating a transparent view of the shared supply network and offering fast and effective support for the crucial decisions to be taken.

The basic elements of the environment are: (a) the decision problem, (b) the quantitative model, (c) the decision support environment (including a user interface) and (d) the data management environment. This last aspect will not be discussed in the context of this paper.

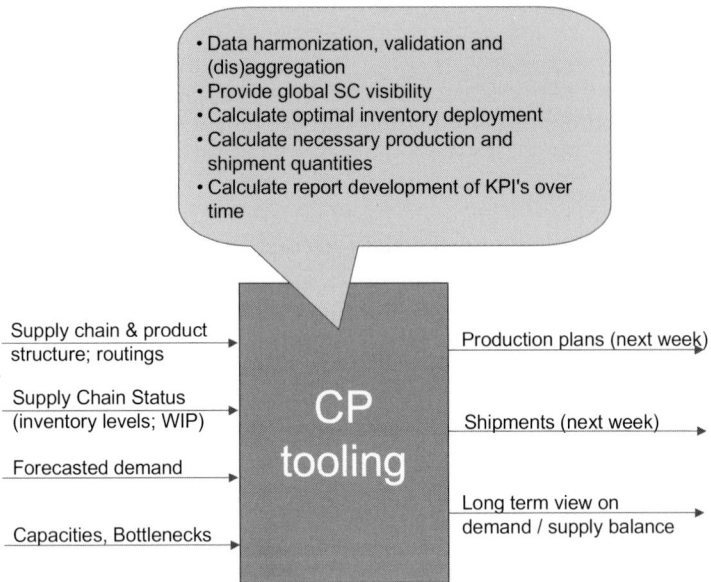

Figure 4: Decision Support System outline for CP

a) The *decision problem* may be (very briefly) stated as follows: co-ordinate the material flows through the supply network in such a way that demand and supply plans are matched in the most profitable way and taking into account decisions on (safety) stock levels and capacity constraints.

b) We have based our *quantitative model* and algorithms on hierarchical planning concepts for multi-echelon inventory systems (see e.g. Diks and De Kok 1998). This leads to a so-called modified base-stock policy approach which enables the rapid calculation of appropriate order releases throughout the network and provides, through a forward and backward pegging mechanism (for the allocation of supply quantities to demand and vice versa), the detailed information to identify and solve bottlenecks.

c) This modelling and solving approach provides the basis for fast and effective calculations. Effective in the sense that within the constraints posed by the network, materials are provided in a synchronised (on time) and balanced manner (in the right quantities). A powerful graphical user interface developed in close co-operation with the actual users complements the *decision support environment*.

4. Case description: how has this been implemented

4.1 Phases in the implementation history

In the project six phases can be distinguished:

1. *History*. Prior to our involvement, the partners had made a first step towards a collaborative relationship. In weekly telephone conference calls, the state of affairs was discussed, and decisions with regard to next week's actions were made. However, the information used in the conference calls was packed in various hard to read and often inconsistent spreadsheets, and the discussion focused on 'fire fighting' rather than on 'proactive decision making'. As a consequence, supply chain performance was rather poor and the trust between the partners was low. The feeling grew with participants and their management that formalisation of a truly collaborative process –with a supporting DSS environment– was badly needed.

2. *Initiating workshops*. As a first step, a number of joint workshops were organised. These workshops focused on the clarification of supply chain and product structures and the planning processes to control these structures. Moreover, a mutual understanding of issues and goals was developed. Both operational planners and their managers were closely involved. An important observation was that, while the project team was struggling with describing and defining their joint business and supply chain, the level of trust increased. The phase concluded with the decision to start a pilot phase for a simple part of the supply chain, i.e. involving a single product through a part of the physical supply chain. In a pilot phase the envisioned collaboration process would have to be introduced and tested, and the first prototype of a supporting decision support system (a DSS based on supply chain analysis concepts, models and algorithms already available) was to be introduced.

3. *Pilot.* In the pilot phase the team concentrated on developing and introducing the DSS, defining processes for collecting all relevant data from the operational systems, and on defining and introducing the 'weekly cycle'. This was a structured process aiming at synchronising the material flows -in a weekly heartbeat- through the whole supply chain. Another aspect of trust was that during this phase, the first signs of the world-wide downturn in PC business appeared. It took the planners four weeks to really trust the figures presented by the DSS and to react according to the decision proposals. This resulted in high stock levels (which was bad) and the recognition that the tooling proposals were correct (which was good). The pilot was concluded with the decisions that yes, the tooling and the process were promising, and yes, the companies needed to proceed with a further roll-out of both process and tooling.

4. *Blueprinting.* Before going ahead it was decided to insert a *blueprinting phase*. A high level view on the *total* supply chain and its planning processes were developed, a business case -summarising expected costs and benefits- was drafted, and the project approach was defined. To assess organisational support for the CP process a survey was conducted with the key stakeholders from the two partners involved in the collaborative planning study. Amongst others, the following questions were asked, to be answered on a five point scale, ranging from 1 = strongly disagree to 5 = strongly agree.

Question	Partner 1 (n=4)	Partner 2 (n=4)	Total (n=8)
I think that collaborative planning will generate mutual benefits	4.5	2.8	3.6
I think that collaborative planning will improve supply chain performance	3.8	3.8	3.8
Do you feel that the theoretical concept of Collaborative Planning matches the practical day to day business environment	5.0	3.8	4.4
In your perception, does Collaborative Planning address the relevant business issues?	4.8	4.4	4.4

Table 2: Selected survey results from blueprinting phase

Though there are some differences between the partners on individual questions, the general conclusion was that there was a high confidence that CP would indeed be beneficial to both parties. This contrasted strongly with the relatively low levels of trust and transparency observed with many of the stakeholders prior to the CP project.

5. The *Proof of Concept* phase aimed at proving that collaborative planning would also work on a larger scale. Proving implied getting positive answers to the following questions: Is the DSS robust and powerful enough? Can we get all the data? Are people (planners, supply chain managers) willing to co-operate? Is it feasible to squeeze the weekly decision making process into a 2-hour virtual meeting? Can we link the CP process to all other processes? Does it bring the value we expect it to bring? Can we find a reasonable rule for sharing supply chain related costs & benefits?
    During this phase, the concept of 'collaborative planning' was introduced at a much wider scale than before. The consequence was that quite some 'new' people needed to be brought on board. Workshops were instrumental for getting the necessary buy-in. When it comes to 'travail': as in any project where software is developed using prototyping, there were the occasional ups and downs in appreciation of the tooling being developed: 'peaks' when new functionality became available in rapid successions; 'downs' when some things proved more difficult to develop or transfer than expected.

6. After a successfull conclusion of the Proof of Concept phase, the project entered the '*maturity*' phase: objective of this phase was a further maturation of the tooling (scalability, sustainability, maintainability), a further roll out of the CP process (more business lines, more components) and a fine-tuning of the process. Where the previous phases had a *business* rather than an *IT* focus, now the further development of the IT environment consumed most resources. From our Travail/Trust/Transparency viewpoint, this phase was rather uneventful, and it gradually passed into the – current – *operational* phase.

At the time of writing, the beginning of 2002, we have a running collaborative planning process executed by the supply chain partners, there is an almost full transparency of the integral supply chain has been created, and the important weekly decisions are truly joint ones. In the design of the weekly process an 'escalation' step had been included. This step – involving senior management – aimed at solving problems that couldn't be solved by the operational planners. The fact that during the entire project this road was never taken, demonstrates that the partners have reached a situation where they have moved from fire-fighting, discussions on correctness of figures and under-performance, have come to a effective 'working together' relationship.

5. Case analysis: interactions of travail, transparency and trust

As could be grasped the previous section, this case largely confirmed the ex ante research model that we had developed on the basis of the existing literature. In this section, we look at *new* aspects of the dynamics of transparency and trust that we had not anticipated beforehand. In particular, we found four aspects of this case especially informative:

5.1 Data transparency alone is not enough

In the very early stages of the project, significant amounts of data (forecasts, inventories, pipeline stocks) *were* exchanged between the customer and supplier; far more than what one would expect in an average customer / supplier relation. At the same time, the level of trust that existed between these parties was relatively low.

One of the root causes for this lack of trust was a lack of understanding for each other's planning processes and, even more, for each other businesses. For instance: a high volatility in forecasts was initially suspected to be the result of 'playing games'. In fact, that volatility was the consequence of market dynamics, and the flexible MPS (master production schedule) processes that were set up to accommodate those dynamics.

5.2 Workshops are an effective means for "travail", for getting virtuous cycles started

Only after spending a number of workshops, focused on explaining businesses, processes, and systems, a mutual understanding for each other's perceived volatility (or rigidity) did materialise. The essence of these workshops lay in creating an additional level of transparency: not on the down-to-earth data level (what do you expect to be able produce in the near future) but at a higher level: *How* do you plan? *Why* do you do it that way? *Who* are involved? Creating this level of transparency significantly contributed to creating trust. And also: creating this level of transparency involved a great deal of *travail*; it was certainly not self-evident to create the open atmosphere that encouraged the organisations to open up to each other.

5.3 Developing and feeding the DSS also is a form of travail, generating trust

A major activity during the project was the development of tooling (a DSS and a supporting data management infrastructure) supporting the CP process. The tooling not only provided the required transparency, but also provided the analytical and number-crunching capabilities needed to get an efficient and effective decision making process; a process that to a large extent centred around a weekly (virtual) meeting in which decisions for the imminent weeks were taken. Again, creating the transparency needed involved lots of travail: getting data of approximately 10 organisational entities turned out to be a laborious undertaking; not only in terms of systems development, but also in terms of getting people and organisations 'on board'.

5.4 Collaboration needs to take place at multiple organisational levels

When it comes to the Trust > Communication > Habituation cycle: during the project communication took place at many managerial levels: at the start, -during the telephone conference- only the operational planners were involved; based on *their* experiences the feeling grew that things needed to be done differently: too many data, while at the same time insufficient true transparency, too many discussions on the *quality* of those data, but also excess stocks and lost sales. The supply chain managers and general managers who initiated the project played an important role here. At this managerial level, prior to the project, there was already a certain degree of habituation and trust. This helped to get the operational people involved in the workshops that, over time, built trust at this level as well.

6. Discussion and conclusion

6.1 Reflection: Trust and transparency are generated by hard work

To a large extent, this study has confirmed empirically the validity of existing strands of theory regarding trust and transparency. In particular, it has supported the notion of the self-reinforcing feedback loops between these key aspects of supply chain collaboration as identified by Akkermans et al. (1999) and De Jong and Noteboom (2000). This in itself may be seen a valid contribution to the literature, as both these earlier research efforts called for empirical validation of their theoretical propositions.

What this research has revealed or at least emphasised is the importance of what we have called travail, of plain honest hard work by all parties involved, in generating the habituation between parties that drives trust and transparency. It is this hard work that, in this case at least, changed a situation of relatively low levels of trust and transparency into one where a virtuous cycle of increasing levels of trust, transparency and supply chain performance could be entered into.

But, one can ask, what is needed to get this travail started? Here there can be many answers. Akkermans et al. (1999) suggested as potential reversals into a virtuous cycle: learning from the success of effective newcomers, demanding customers and visionary managers. To some extent, all these favourable conditions and more were, in retrospect, present in this particular case.

6.2   Limitations and follow-up opportunities

Obviously, this was a single case study and so the generalisability of our findings remains limited. Therefore, an obvious follow-up research effort would be to evaluate multiple collaborative planning settings in a similar manner and generalise on the basis of a cross-case analysis of these.

Also, it might be beneficial to translate the research model presented here into a quantified simulation model to explore with more rigour the various dynamic patterns of behaviour that are possible in such a causal structure, which is also recommended by De Jong and Noteboom (2000). As with collaborative planning, quite some research travail will be needed before sufficient transparency is established in this complex but fascinating matter.

6.3   Managerial implications

Theoretically, many questions remain. But, managerially speaking, the implications from this study are straightforward: Supply chain collaboration is essential to prosper in many of today's volatile markets. Collaborative planning is an advanced form of such collaboration, which requires seamless joint work flows, "open kimono" attitude (show all the info and knowledge you have attitude) at all parties, tailored IT support and knowledgeable and trusting supply chain professionals. But, first of al, before such a situation can be reached, it requires a lot of hard work from the people involved. They will only engage in such an arduous task if they are convinced that they have the full backing of their senior management. It is here that, even in today's highly decentralised organisational settings, managers still can and have to play a leading part.

6.4 Conclusions

Supply chain collaboration is more important than ever. It requires high levels of trust and information transparency on all sides. Here OR algorithms and decision support systems can provide essential support. However, what this study has stressed is that, to achieve the levels of transparency needed to make these algorithms and systems work, high levels of trust are required. And, that such levels of trust and transparency can be attained only by a great deal of hard work, or *travail* as we have called it, by all people involved. Once this is accomplished, supply chain partners will find themselves in a virtuous cycle of steadily improving supply chain performance leading to even higher levels of trust and transparency, which in turn will improve performance even further.

Meanwhile, collaborative planning remains an especially advanced form of supply chain collaboration, in which multiple independent companies take joint decisions on production and shipments for large parts of their collective supply chain. At the time of writing, no one is really sure of how such *collaborative planning* settings should really be designed but that, at the same time, the improvement potential of such collaboration seems very great. This case study of collaborative planning in a high-tech electronics supply chain has shown that, probably regardless of the specific design chosen, crucial roles are played by the concepts of travail, transparency and trust.

7. References

Akkermans, H.A./Bogerd, P./Vos, B. (1999), "Virtuous and vicious cycles on the road towards international supply chain management", International Journal of Operations and Production Management, Vol. 19, No. 5/6, pp.565-581.

Aviv, Y. (2001), "The effect of collaborative forecasting on supply chain performance", Management Science, 47(10), pp. 1326-1343.

Cachon, G.P./Fisher, M. (2000), "Supply Chain Inventory Management and the Value of Shared Information", Management Science, 46(8), pp. 1032-1048.

Christopher, M. (1992), *Logistics and Supply Chain Management*. Financial Times Pitman Publishing, London.

De Jong, G./Nooteboom, B. (2000), *The causal structure of long-term supply relationships.* Kluwer Academic Publishers, Boston.

Diks, E.B./De Kok, A.G. (1998), "Optimal control of a divergent n-echelon inventory system", European Journal of Operations Research, 111, pp. 75-97.

Fine, C.H. (1998), *Clockspeed: Winning Industry Control in the Age of Temporary Advantage.* Perseus Books.

Forrester, J.W. (1961), *Industrial dynamics,* Cambridge MA: MIT Press.

Lee, H./Padmanabhan, P./Whang, S. (1997), "Information Distortion in a Supply Chain: The Bullwhip Effect", Management Science, 43(4) , pp. 516-558

Raghunathan, S. (1999), "Interorganizational collaborative forecasting and replenishment systems and supply chain implication", Decision Sciences, 30(4), pp. 1053-1071.

Sherman, R.J. (1998), "Collaborative planning, forecasting & replenishment (CPFR): realising the promise of efficient customer response through collaborative technology", Journal of Marketing Theory and Practice, 6(4), pp. 6-9.

Sterman, J.D. (2000). *Business dynamics: Systems thinking and modeling for a complex world,* McGraw-Hill, New York.

8.

ILC SCAN: Lessons from ILC Business Cases

Thierry Verduijn, Menno Rustenburg (TNO Inro)
Frans-Peter Scheer (ATO)

Abstract

Many organizations struggle with the question of how they can optimize their supply chain activities in order to strengthen their competitive position. Regarding their relationships with suppliers and customers, they need to find out whether and how collaborative planning can be beneficial for them and how to design and realize this collaboration with their supply chain partners. This chapter aims to assist organizations in their 'quest' for an efficient and effective collaboration with their partners. We propose a method that can be used as a quick scan to analyse the opportunities of improving supply chain activities through collaborative planning. The method is based on experiences from eight business cases in which the opportunities of Intelligent Logistics Concepts have been explored. These business cases provide insight in the aspects that play a crucial role in the development of an Intelligent Logistics Concept.

I. Introduction

Intelligent Logistics Concepts (ILC) are innovative logistics concepts that allow organizations to improve their inter-organizational co-ordination through collaborative planning. ILC consists of three layers (see also chapter 2). Connectivity among supply chain partners facilitates the efficient exchange of electronic data. Transparency is the mutual openness by supply chain partners with respect to specific transaction, planning and status information. It allows organizations to get a wider and better view on what is going on in the supply chain by exchanging essential information on the planning and status of logistics processes. Together, connectivity and transparency provide the basis for closer supply chain co-ordination, especially with respect to the design and planning of supply chain processes.

Many organizations struggle with the issue of whether and how collaborative planning can be beneficial for them and how to design and realize this collaboration with their supply chain partners. To answer the first question, knowledge is required on what forms of ILC exist, what factors determine their success and in what situations they can be used.

Furthermore, in order to find out in whether collaborative planning can be beneficial to an organization or the supply chain, instruments are needed to support organizations in identifying their performances and the type of ILC that is appropriate for their circumstances. For the second question, which refers to the process of designing and implementing an ILC, essential process steps need to be identified to get collaboration established. In scientific literature, there are still few analyses of the process of designing and implementing supply chain collaboration and planning (see also chapter 7).

The design and implementation of supply chain collaboration is a complicated task. In the exploration of the opportunities and benefits and design of the collaboration, issues such as joint decision-making, increased dependencies, trust, changes to internal processes and sharing of costs and benefits have to be addressed. In the implementation phase, the topics of financing, selection and adjustment of information and communication systems and change management play a significant role. A tool can be useful for identifying, assessing and evaluating each of these aspects systematically and coherently. Unfortunately, there are few tools freely available and these elaborate only on the opportunities brought by the concept of Collaborative Planning Forecasting and Replenishment (CPFR).

The objective of this chapter is to support organizations with the identification and development of a wider range of potential applications of collaborative planning. To this end we set a first step towards a generic ILC SCAN. This ILC SCAN helps organizations to identify potential improvements, to identify essential interdependencies in the processes and co-ordination and to select and refine a concept for collaborative planning. This proposed tool consists of a description of some basic forms of ILC on the one hand and of a process description how such an exploration and development can be conducted, on the other.

To develop the tool, we analyse the results of eight business cases that have been completed within the ILC program. In each of these business cases, the opportunities of ILC have been explored. The business cases provide insight into the various aspects and choice in the development of an ILC and the steps that were taken to gain these insights. Furthermore, the analysis of the business cases provides an overview of the research that has taken place within the ILC research program. The examples may inspire organizations to develop their own ILC.

The outline of this paper is as follows. Section 2 quickly reviews the scans developed for CFPR and VMI, which are freely available on the Internet. Section 3 discusses the research approach and presents the eight business cases. In section 4, a more in-depth analysis of business cases is presented. Section 5 presents some generalized insights of forms of Intelligent Logistics Concepts. Section 6 presents a step-wise approach to the identification of opportunities of ILC in the supply chain.

2. Scans for collaborative planning

In supply chain and logistics management many scans have been developed for the analysis of supply chain operations and the identification of bottlenecks and improvements. These tools consists of classification of supply chain situations and related strategies, questionnaires to determine what situation a firm is in, step-by-step methodologies that describe and explain the process of analysis and design, performance measurements and process mapping tools that help to summarize and structure the complexities. Many consultants and research institutes use a tool kit of instruments that have been developed and refined over time. Only a few instruments are freely available and can be used by supply chain partners themselves. The number of collaborative planning tools is limited. On the Internet we found only two tools that are especially designed for and focused on collaborative planning.

The first tool was developed by ICT consultancy firm Involation (Involation, 2002) and is used as pre-test to determine whether the application of collaborative planning in the supply chain of an organization is likely to result in supply chain benefits. The test addresses two dimensions: the impact on supply chain performance and the feasibility of implementation in the supply chain. For each dimension five questions must be answered. By combining the two scores, an initial assessment of the appropriateness of the concepts can be read from a table. The advice provided by the table ranges from: 'Although there is much potential for improvement by means of integration, you need to improve your internal processes and co-ordination first' to 'Start immediately! There is much to improve and it is really possible to seize the opportunity!' In its current form, the tool is primarily a marketing tool. It is used by Involation to trigger organizations to consider supply chain collaboration more seriously. To really assist organizations in their quest for supply chain collaboration, the questionnaire needs to be extended and guide organizations more thoroughly to a form of collaboration that fits their situation.

A much more extensive analysis tool has been developed by the VICS (1999). A detailed nine-step approach describes how the concept of CPFR should be used and how a seller and manufacturer should cooperate to forecast, plan en replenish jointly. A CPFR roadmap is presented to help organizations explore the opportunities of CPFR and to assist them on the road from awareness of CPFR opportunities to drawing up implementation plans. Based on the CPFR process model, it aligns the initiating organization and its trading partner to common objectives and guides them together through forecast exchange, exception management and the review of performance results. The roadmap contains five steps: evaluate current conditions, define scope and objectives, prepare for collaboration, execute and assess results and identify improvements.

To support the evaluation of the current situation, the Roadmap presents a CPFR Capability assessment in the form of a grid. The grid provides an overview of progression on the activities through each CPFR process area. The grid illustrates the increasing difficulty and benefit progressing vertically through the processes of Collaboration (A) to Integrated Planning and Forecasting (B) to Replenishment Processes (C) and finally Supply Chain Optimization (D). In each of these core competencies organizations should move from basic to advanced levels. The ultimate goal of CPFR is Supply Chain Optimization, which is possible only if advanced levels are achieved for every process area. A total of 18 individually scored criteria have been defined to enable organizations to assess their current situation. Criteria arranged on a five-point scale awards scores on each of the four processes. These scores allow organizations to position themselves in the CPFR grid.

Process Area	Basic	Development	Advanced
D Supply Chain Management	No Supply Chain Focus / Plan	Internal Enterprise Optimization	Supply Chain Optimization
C Replenishment Processes	Pre-DC Limited / No Retail Visibility	DC Replenishment Focus	Computer Assisted Retail Ordering Flow-Through
B Integrated Planning & Forecasting Processes	Manual Non-Standard Forecasting Planning	Standardized Demand Data Creation & Input	Integrated Planning Forecasting & Collaboration
A Collaborative Processes	Limited One-Way Communication	Standardized & Integrated Collaboration	

Figure 1: CPFR stages of progression (VICS, 2002)

3. Approach

CPFR addresses just one of the areas in which organizations can improve their inter-organizational co-ordination of logistics processes. CPFR focuses entirely on co-ordination between inventory management and replenishment in various parts of the supply chain. The CPRF Roadmap does not include or consider other forms or areas of collaboration. Organizations must also improve the co-ordination of other business processes (for example transport and production management or transport and warehouse management) and to improve their logistics performance. A method that supports organizations in exploring and implementing other forms of supply chain collaboration does not yet exist. The aim of this chapter is to present a first step in the development of such a method.

To gain insight into various forms of collaborative planning and how the opportunities of ILC can be identified, several business cases from the ILC research program were analysed. Besides the business cases of the container transport chain of Vos Logistics, the improvements in the fruit supply chain and the design of a decentralized planning concept for barge transport, various other applications of collaborative planning have been explored and developed in the ILC research program. In our analysis, a total of eight case studies were selected in which a total of eleven different potential applications of ILC were identified. Only business cases from which the final report was available were included in this analysis.

In each of the cases studied, the supply chain partners worked closely together with research institutes, business consultants and IT specialists to describe the current supply chain situation, to identify the areas of improvement and to develop an ILC to achieve the supply chain improvement by means of inter-organizational co-ordination and planning. This chapter uses the results of each case study combined with background information available from the research institutes that were involved in the exploration. The results of each case study are described in a business case report. The business cases included in this chapter are presented anonymously in Table 1. The name of each of the cases reveals in what sector the organizations operate. In the cases of Food co and Tulip co, multiple designs of ILC were identified with different levels of complexity and impact on the supply chain. Each design of ILC is indicated with a separate number, e.g. Food co 2. The designs differ in complexity and impact on the supply chain.

Business case	Description
ChemicalCo.	Co-ordination of transport planning and transport tendering and contracting between independent business units of a large chemical firm operating internationally. Integration and connection of ERP systems. The purchase and planning of transport is organized through a combined information system.
FoodCo. 1	Co-ordination of manufacturing planning and transport planning for perishable food products. Digitalizing the exchange of information instead of sending it by fax. Improvement of efficiency in each of the planning departments.
FoodCo. 2	Co-ordination of manufacturing planning and transport planning for perishable food products. Optimization of operational information exchange by using a central database for accepted customer orders and the online availability of planning information.
FoodCo. 3	Co-ordination of manufacturing planning and transport planning for perishable food products. Integration of different planning systems into a joint manufacturing and transport planning process.
TulipCo. 1	Inbound transport of flowers from growers to the auction. Transporters send ETA information to the auction. The auction can plan the resources required for local handling more efficiently. This is done by means of a central datahub.
TulipCo. 2	Through the central datahub, all parties know the ETA information of the transporters beforehand. An optimal warehouse, dock and transport planning can be realized between transporters and with the auction.
BulkCo.	Shippers send ETA information to the Logistical Service Provider. The LSP can plan the use of local resources more efficiently by offering VMI to his customers and replenish inventories when ships are available.
CableCo.	The LSP transports products directly from the factory to the customers and does not use the factory's Country Distribution Centers. The LSP can plan the operational process more efficiently.
AnimalCo.	An LSP wants ETA information and transport status information on suppliers. In this case, the LSP can optimize dock and warehouse planning.
RoseCo.	Redesign of the chain by which the supply chain lead time of 24 hours is reduced to 8 hours. The supply and ordering process is automated and organized by a third party.
ContainerCo.	A central datahub is used for exchange of electronic status information between the LSP, transport operator, shipper and the customer through the Internet. The selected solution is not planning integration, but creates transparency that improves the operational planning of the LSP.

Table 1: selected case studies

The cases show a great variety of different applications and sectors. We have opted for a highly generic approach so as not to hang up the tool on one specific concept, as was the case with CPFR. This implies that rather than selecting detailed classifications, strategies and a questionnaire, we have chosen to describe the method using a number of key ILC characteristics. The ILC Scan tool comprises two elements, the first a content checklist of aspects that form part of every exploratory and developmental process and the second a step-by-step plan of this exploratory and developmental process, indicating when and how these aspects are of consequence.

The development of the tool consists of three steps:

– *Identification of characteristics*: The case studies were described and compared using a list of characteristics. These characteristics include some general aspects of supply chain improvement and supply chain collaboration and are frequently used in supply chain literature and organization theory. The characteristics are presented in section 4.

– *Identification of forms of Intelligent Logistics Concepts:* Based on the designs and characteristics of the Intelligent Logistics Concepts developed in the business cases, three general forms of Intelligent Logistics Concepts are identified. The characteristics are described in section 5.

– *Definition of a scanning tool:* In the third step a scanning procedure was worked out containing four steps that have to be taken to identify the possibilities for chain optimization and to have a general course of realization. These steps, discussed in section 6, are also based on the reports of the different business cases.

4.   Dimensions of Intelligent Logistics Concepts

In this section, a number of characteristics including supply chain co-ordination situations, improvement objectives and nature of the selected solutions are used to compare the business cases. This provides greater insight into the variety of situations in which collaborative planning can contribute towards improving supply chain performance as well as a better understanding of the various forms of co-ordination. The characteristics chosen are: supply chain improvement objectives, business processes, process interdependencies, level of collaboration, forms of co-ordination and information requirements.

Supply Chain improvement objectives

As shown in the literature, collaborative planning can be used to realize a wide range of improvements in the way in which the chain parties can work together to supply the customer with the product. The aim of the collaboration in most of the conducted business cases was to enhance efficiency. In the case of Chemical co, Food co, Tulip co and Container co, the aim was to enlarge capacity utilization degree of transport. Animal co and Tulip co focused on improving loading and unloading as well as warehousing processes. Bulk co indicated that they wish to extend their service provision to customers by applying, among other things, the Vendor Management Inventory. This Inventory allows them to further optimize their transport capacity, in the sense that goods should not only be shipped when they are needed but whenever it is possible to do so. The aim of Cable co is to improve efficiency of the entire chain by leaving out the central supplier's warehouse. The objective set by Rose co was the most ambitious, namely to improve co-ordination in the chain in order to shorten lead times from more than 24 hours to 8 hours. The customer then receives a higher quality product with a longer storage life.

Business processes

The business cases focus on a wide range of business processes and demonstrate that supply chain collaboration can have advantages beyond the co-ordination of ordering patterns and stock management between two organizations. The business cases show the advantages of coordinating the transport processes of various companies (Chemical co), transport and production (Food co), transport and warehousing (Animal co, Tulip co), transport, stock management and transshipment (Bulk co, Cable co), and transport and purchasing (Rose co).

Reciprocal dependencies

Insight into process interdependencies is essential if co-ordination between the various organizational processes is to be achieved. When controlling and managing these processes, this in turn offers a direct insight into the consequences for other processes within the chain. In organization theory, Thompson (1967) distinguishes three different ways in which work of organizational units may be dependent on each other (see Figure 2). First, with pooled dependency, "each part renders a discrete contribution to the whole and each is supported by the whole" (Thompson, 1967)[1]. Second,

---

[1]   Pooled interdependence is also interpreted as units that share and use common resources but are otherwise independent (Kumar & van Dissel, 1996).

sequential interdependence arises when one part, B, depends directly on another part, A. The dependence is asymmetric. Third, in reciprocal dependency parts feed their work back and forth among themselves; in effect, each receives input from and provides output to others, often interactively. If reciprocal interdependence is present, so are the sequential and pooled types. Van de Ven et al (1976) extended the latter form with team interdependence where actors work jointly and simultaneously (see Figure 2).

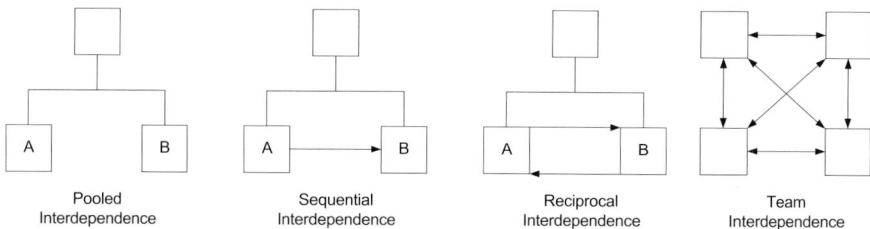

Figure 2: Types of interdependencies (McCann & Galbraith, 1981)

There are two ways in which organizations can depend on each other in a supply chain: in the physical process, the work as recognized by Thompson, and in the provision and co-ordination of information. The dependencies in the physical process are mostly of a sequential nature. The one organization supplies goods to the following party in the chain. This organization cannot come into action until the first has provided the goods. In addition, pooled interdependencies can exist if several organizations need to or wish to use the same facility or resources that is in short supply. In that case, the parties should make clear-cut agreements as to how capacity is to be assigned. Reciprocal relationships also occur if another party has to carry out specific operations on the product before it is returned for further processing. Dependencies also arise when harmonizing the flow of goods or the use of certain resources, as organizations need to receive information from others in order to carry out these tasks efficiently and effectively. In such cases, too, pooled, sequential, reciprocal and team dependencies can be distinguished.

The business cases also display various forms of physical and management dependencies. Pooled interdependence occurs in the business cases of Chemical co and Tulip co in which the actors share a pool of resources. An ILC needs to coordinate how these resources are allocated to the various organizations. The organizations have to define the rules and procedures together since each decision has a direct impact on the other organizations. Sequential interdependencies occur in the cases of Container co and Animal co. In these cases, processes need to be planned and executed based on incoming goods flows that cannot be influenced by the receiving actors. The ILC has to focus on defining and exchanging the information that allows the receiving organizations to improve their processes. Reciprocal planning interdependencies are observed in the case of Rose co. The growers provide information on the availability of goods to a brokering department, which receives orders from a merchant and places purchasing orders to the growers. The growers, in turn, deliver the flowers to the merchant. In the case of reciprocal interdependency, the performance of this process depends on information exchange. In situations of reciprocal dependencies, the scenarios and speed of the information exchange process are key issues of an ILC. A form of team interdependency can be observed in the business case of Food co. Since orders from customers come in very late, manufacturing and transport planning departments are planning the orders at the same time. However, currently the orders are planned independently by the two departments, which basically means that the two departments involved plan sequentially and transport planning cannot influence the moment at which the shipments become available for transport and hardly has any opportunity to optimize its resources or find additional loads.

Level of collaboration

The supply chain improvement objectives, as well as the processes and the dependencies are important indicators of the level of decision-making at which co-ordination takes place between the parties. Here we distinguish between strategic, tactical and operational levels. Taking place for the most part at an operational level, co-ordination is required to plan daily processes more efficiently and to ensure a better match between these processes in terms of realization. Examples are Container co, Tulip co and Animal co. The processes and resources as such do not change as a result of this. At a tactical level, parties adapt their resources and process to improve effectiveness and efficiency. In the case of Food co, the producer may decide to refuse overdue orders that have led to high transport costs or to levy an additional transport charge. Chemical co is coordinating contracts between carriers and their joint transport requirements. Bulk co is changing the way in which their shipping capacity is planned and the moment at which cargo is transported. At the strategic level, the structure of the chain and the assignment of the tasks to be carried out also changes. Rose co are looking for other mechanisms of managing the chain and hence introducing a number of structural changes. To achieve a high level of collaboration and a major ILC impact organizations are required to have full confidence in each other and ensure that their relationship is one of close cooperation. This is especially the case where significant investments are needed to realize ILC.

New co-ordination concept for logistical processes and the related information
The essence of an Intelligent Logistics Concept is to improve management, i.e. planning and co-ordination between processes in the supply chain. In business cases in which new forms of co-ordination have to be initiated, the first step is that each of the parties has to make an individual attempt to use current information supplied by others to improve their planning. Collaboration here is limited to making information available to others, the planning itself is not yet adjusted at this stage. A case in point is Container co – the party receiving the information can improve the transport capacity. Although transparency is enhanced, optimization is still localized. We call this form of co-ordination one-sided.

A second step is to create a round of co-ordination in the planning, such that where this leads to sub-optimum situations, each chain party has the opportunity of adjusting their individual planning in reaction to or at the request of other parties. For instance in the case of Tulip co, a carrier can decide to change its time of arrival at the auction if long queues are expected at loading and unloading docks. We call this type of co-ordination sequential co-ordination.

In a number of cases resources are used more efficiently if they are jointly planned. This is the most advanced form of collaborative planning. The ultimate goal of Food co is to establish integrated or joint planning, in which the parties decide jointly how best to coordinate production and transport planning.

We conclude that 'real' joint planning is not yet a reality in most business cases. Although most organizations acknowledge the desirability of concerted planning, it goes a step too far for most of them. To achieve this, they have to invest in close relationships and create stronger IT systems, and that is only worthwhile if collaborating with others is also of strategic importance to them (Bensaou, 1997).

The demands on information provision
The nature of the logistics management concept that underlies ILC makes certain demands on information and information systems. Depending on the process involved, the availability of information and the current patterns of information exchange, emphasis can be on:

– accuracy – is the information correct, reliable, precise and relevant? To what extent are exact details required or is an overall picture or estimate enough?
– availability and comprehensiveness – is the information available and complete, and have all chain parties supplied the information they need? (transparency)
– punctuality – was the information received at the correct moment?
– destination of planning information – are all parties involved in a position to send and receive the information? (connectivity)

In some business cases, processes in which, to date, no conformity existed have now been coordinated. Availability of information is a first step in these cases (Animal co, Tulip co, Chemical co, Cable co and Bulk co). In a number of other cases, creating an optimum and comprehensive body of information is an important step (Container co). Punctuality is the most important aspect for Rose co and Food c. Planning processes have to be completed quickly to shorten lead times or to synchronize two concurrent planning processes. Where that is concerned, a process of real-time information exchange is essential. Most parties tried to find an IT solution with a joint database. Where two-party collaboration is concerned, this is a relatively simple solution, but where more parties are involved this can be very difficult.

   In summary, it can be said that the development of an ILC involves the following six questions or dimensions:

– What improvement objective is to be achieved with ILC?
– Which business processes have to be coordinated?
– In which way are these functions interdependent?
– What is the scope of ILC and what impact does it have on the supply chain ?
– Which type of co-ordination is best for harmonizing these processes?
– What kind of information needs to be exchanged and what requirements does it have to meet?

Table 2 presents an overview of all the characteristics of each business case. The table emphasizes the variety of situations in which collaborative planning can be beneficial and the variety of forms that can be applied.

	supply chain improvement	business processes	interdependency	level of collaboration	coordination concept	information requirements
chemical co	increase efficiency of resources	transport	pooled resource sharing	tactical	pooled resources	completeness, shared information system
food co 1	increase efficiency of resources	transport & manufacturing	team simultaneous planning	operational	improved independent planning	timeliness, seperate information systems
food co 2	increase efficiency of resources	transport & manufacturing	team simultaneous planning	operational	improved independent planning	completeness, timeliness, shared information system
food co 3	increase efficiency of resources	transport & manufacturing	team simultaneous planning	tactical	joint integrated planning	completeness, timeliness, shared information system
tulip co 1	increase efficiency of resources	transport & warehousing	sequential planning	operational	improved independent planning	completeness; shared information system
tulip co 2	increase efficiency of resources	transport & warehousing	pooled source sharing	strategic	pooled resources, integrated planning	completeness; shared information system
bulk co 1	improve customer service	transport, inventory & terminal operations	sequential	operational	improved resource planning	completeness
cable co	increase responsiveness	customer service & maintenance	sequential	operational	improved task planning	completeness
animal co	increase efficiency of resources	transport & warehousing	reciprocal	operational	improved independent planning	timeliness, completeness
rose co	reduce supply chain lead time	transport & sales	reciprocal	strategic	redesign supply chain processes	timeliness, completeness
container co	increase efficiency of resources	transport & terminal operations	sequential	operational	improved independent planning	timeliness, completeness

Table 2: overview of the characteristics of the business cases

5. Forms and effects of ILC

So far, various characteristics have been used to analyse the business cases. Three generic forms of co-ordination have been discussed – one-sided, sequential and integrated or joint co-ordination. The cases show that each kind of co-ordination sets different requirements on the various layers of an ILC, i.e. connectivity, transparency and planning/network design. The table below gives a brief interpretation of the layers connectivity, transparency and network design & management with respect to each form of co-ordination.

	One-sided planning	Sequential planning	Integrated planning
Network Design & Management	Local planning tools	Dynamic planning tools	Integral planning tools
	Local performance indicators	Local performance indicators	Joint performance indicators
Transparency	Agreements about confidentiality and accessibility of data	Procedures/scenarios information exchange (timeliness)	Joint development of information flows and databases
Connectivity	Web site status EDI-messages	Standard messages – EDI Datahub	Integration/ interfacing of planning systems

Table 3: forms of ILC

One-sided planning

Where co-ordination is one-sided, one of the chain parties provides more information regarding logistic planning and decision-making in other organizations. Simple web sites and other interfaces can be used (connectivity) to make this information available. Parties requiring information about the status of a process, or about planning or shipment can find this information on web sites. Well-known examples are the status information provided by companies such as DHL and UPS, or packages and home delivery planning that a company such as Praxis makes known through a web site. Direct exchange of this information between the chain parties' information systems is also possible. Most suppliers of ICT logistic systems have interfaces or platforms for this purpose. The essence of this type of co-ordination lies in transparency. Organizations are not always interested in providing other chain parties with logistic information. The recipient may benefit from using the information, but the provider is often left with nothing but the costs. Among the motives for incurring costs and providing information may be close commercial collaborations, quality of service provision and a competitive edge within the chain or sector. Local planning occurs at the level of network management & design. The information recipient is in a position to improve his or her planning or processes. Planning between two parties is not harmonized. Because more information is made available, planning tools may have to be adjusted or extended in order to make better use of this information. Local performance measures suffice, given that each party continues to do its own planning.

Sequential planning

Sequential co-ordination involves the provision of information by one of the chain parties, planning by another organization and a feedback loop which informs the first organisation of the planning results. This, in turn, enables the first organization to adjust its planning accordingly. The Tulip co business case is a case in point. If all carriers specify when they expect to arrive at the auction, the latter can set up a cross-dock planning and provide further information in response to this feedback at which point each of the trucks can be dealt with. If, on account of peak load, this point in time varies greatly from the original time set by the carrier, the carrier can adjust transport planning. As this means sending information to and fro over a short period of time, the demands made on information provision are much higher. The information has to be updated constantly. As such, the same solutions can be used as in one-side co-ordination. Where transparency is concerned, more clarification will be needed as to the way in which information is exchanged and when each of the parties needs it. Responsibility for planning is still local. Dynamic planning tools can be used if there is a constant stream of new information. Each party makes its own decisions and will be able to identify the improvements using performance measurements. A joint decision regarding performance measures is advisable once collaboration becomes more intense and the costs and benefits are settled between the parties.

Integrated or joint planning

Where co-ordination takes place jointly, planning is integrated. The relevant information supplied by both parties should be combined in a single system. The information in the information systems needs to be synchronized in real time at the point of decision-making or planning. Transparency has to be at a maximum when planning takes place jointly. In most cases, the essence lies in the development of a new planning tool that can integrate the various objectives and criteria of both parties. An example of such a tool is given in Chapter 5. Once planning has more bearing on the support of daily and operational processes, the requirements in terms of information that the system has to meet will be higher. Fast and effective interfaces will then be needed.

A further dimension we have not yet mentioned involves the number of parties in an Intelligent Logistics Concept that are involved in the design of an ILC system. In some business cases we note co-ordination between two organizations, i.e. a 1:1 relationship. Both parties are required to agree on which information is to be exchanged, in which way and how it is to be used to achieve co-ordination. However, for several logistic chains, the advantages will only become a reality if the organizations are able to realize improved co-ordination with all or at least with the most important supply chain partners (1:N or N:1 relationships). Where both suppliers and buyers, as well as shippers and carriers are involved, as is the case with Container co and Tulip co, this means coordinating an N:N relationship. This situation can, of course, still be solved using interfaces. But where data exchange processes and data requirements have been clearly defined, using concepts such as that of the datahub (see Chapter 3) is both an efficient and an effective option as they make it possible to combine a generic data structure with multi-party exchange. A datahub is especially suitable for one-sided and sequential co-ordination situations. In most cases, integrated or joint planning is difficult to achieve if there is no powerful party in the network. Cases such as Tulip co, Container co and the Approach project (see Chapter 6) show that in N:N co-ordination situations in particular, the desire to retain autonomy makes it difficult to achieve integrated planning.

6. ILC Scan: step-by-step plan

So far, the analysis of the business cases has focused on the characteristics of the ILC and the forms of ILC that can be observed in the business cases. But the proof of the pudding is in the eating. Organizations should be able to identify the characteristics of their supply chain situation and to select a form of ILC. As a result of the approach taken in the business cases, a generic ILC Scan has been developed. This scan consists of a step-by-step plan to help chain parties to gain greater insight into the way the chain is currently functioning. It also helps to recognize opportunities for improving logistics processes with the help of collaborative planning and to select a form of co-ordination with which to realize these improvements. The tool cannot provide a full analysis of the way in which an ILC solution can or should be applied – it roughly suggests a course of development.

The ILC Scan comprises four steps:

1. Strategic focus of collaboration and supply chain improvements;

2. Identification of ILC opportunities and functional design of ILC;

3. Identification of a development path;

4. Overall design and choice of IT logistics service provider.

Each phase involves input, transformation and an output. The input indicates what information is needed in this step. The transformation indicates what kind of analyses should be performed to obtain the required insights and outcomes. The step-by-step plan can be schematically represented as follows:

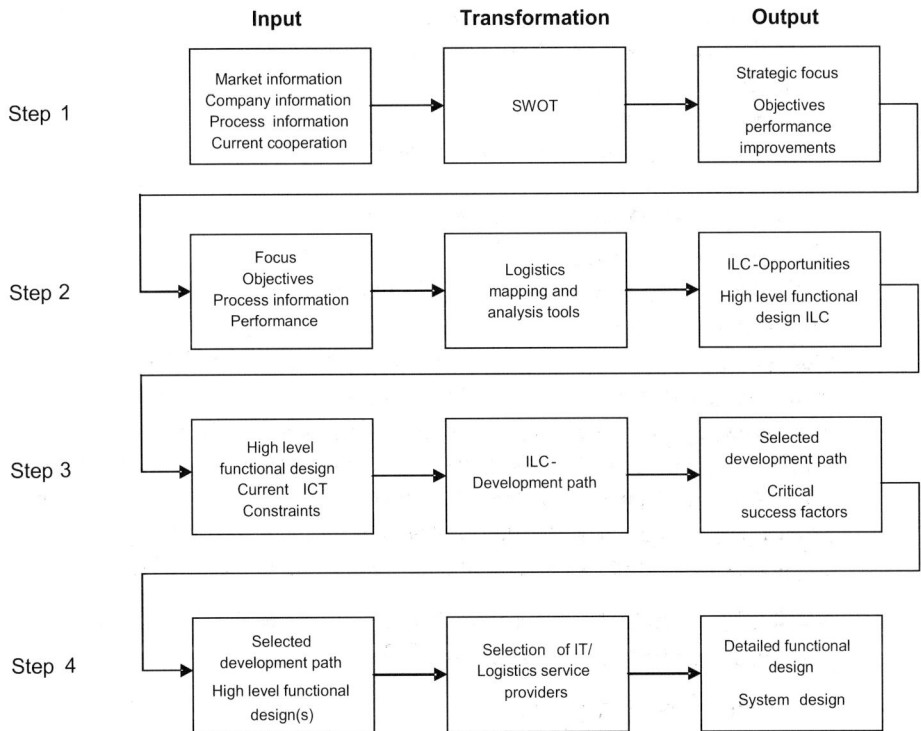

	Input	Transformation	Output
Step 1	Market information Company information Process information Current cooperation	SWOT	Strategic focus Objectives performance improvements
Step 2	Focus Objectives Process information Performance	Logistics mapping and analysis tools	ILC-Opportunities High level functional design ILC
Step 3	High level functional design Current ICT Constraints	ILC-Development path	Selected development path Critical success factors
Step 4	Selected development path High level functional design(s)	Selection of IT/Logistics service providers	Detailed functional design System design

Figure 3: Steps of the ILC SCAN

Step 1: Strategic focus

Step 1 charts the strategic importance of an ILC – known otherwise as chain co-ordination – for an organization or logistics chain, the crux being to establish to what extent and in which way effective logistics contribute towards the total performance of a supply chain. Improved logistic co-ordination can be important in realizing higher service levels, lower operational cost, higher margins and, ultimately, a better competitive position of the organizations involved and the supply chain as a whole.

A traditional SWOT analysis may be used to determine the strategic focus required to develop an ILC. Each of the organizations singly can use the SWOT analysis to analyse itself, but they can use it jointly with a view to the intended collaboration. The analysis helps to explain the strengths and weaknesses of the chain parties, i.e. which logistic processes are conducted and managed effectively or otherwise, and which opportunities or risks occur in and around the organization or the logistics chain (market, customers, competitors, technology) in question.

The strategic focus is then used to define the objectives (and the evaluation criteria) for improving performance. These objectives can be expressed in terms of the reduction of order lead time, higher capacity utilization or loading degree, the reduction of waiting times, etc.

Step 2: Identification of ILC opportunities

The aim of the second step of the ILC Scan is to identify forms of Intelligent Logistics Concepts that can be used to bring about the desired improvements in performance. The first important step is to get a thorough and detailed idea of current processes, management, information streams and performance levels of each organization involved. At this stage, standard logistic analysis tools such as process diagram technologies, Pareto analyses, etc., can be used. The description of the logistics processes of each organization forms the starting point of an analysis of the management of processes beyond the organization itself. The following are important questions used to identify potential improvements in co-ordination:

–   What interactions and dependencies are there between the various logistics processes and decisions?

–   Which time-critical and information-critical processes can be identified in planning realization?

–   What are the most important disruptive factors in realizing planning and performing processes?

–   What is the importance for and the expected effect of improvements on the provision of punctual, complete and correct information on managing logistic process?

–   In addition to transaction information (orders and invoices), what information is electronically exchanged, i.e. status overviews and planning details, and for which processes?

Having answered the above questions, the most appropriate form of co-ordination can now be characterized using three co-ordination concepts:

•   one-sided co-ordination: making information available for improving logistics planning for chain partners;

•   sequential co-ordination: exchanging information with chain partners in such a way that each can improve on individual planning and optimize co-ordination with others;

•   integrated co-ordination: joint planning or high-frequency planning co-ordination so that processes blend seamlessly with one another.

As reciprocal dependencies increase and the importance and impact of collaborations enhance competitive position, integrated planning will increasingly become an option.

Step 3: Identification of the development path
The aim of step 3 is to determine which changes are needed to move from the current 'Ist' situation to the desired 'Soll' situation. Where the 'Ist' situation is concerned, the analysis of information flows from step 2 is extended to include an analysis of the information and communication systems present in the chain. A number of characteristics of various co-ordination types explained in the previous section are intended for the 'Soll'. However large the improvement potential is, the jump from no co-ordination to comprehensive integration is either unwelcome or even impossible for several organizations. These organizations often prefer to start by sounding out the collaboration partner and building a basis of trust before opting for intense collaboration. Investments in ICT and adjustments to the organization can be substantial, making a phased approach more advisable. Moreover, organizations can only process a limited number of changes in one go as they have to maintain the continuity of operational processes.

Alternatively, organizations can opt for a development path. This path would then comprise a series of smaller steps, bringing about a small(er) improvement at each stage. The arrows in Table 4 show which development paths are possible. Depending on the ILC type (column), connectivity is a condition for transparency and transparency a condition for improved planning and co-ordination. Seen horizontally, organizations can grow from one-sided co-ordination towards integrated planning. At each step the complexity of the co-ordination, the intensity of the collaboration and the demands made on information provision increase. Integration and joint planning is, incidentally, not a necessity in every case – one-sided co-ordination can, in certain scenarios, lead to a sufficient level of improvement. A growth path can only be successful if future wishes and requirements are taken into consideration in the design and implementation of ICT support systems.

	One-sided planning	Sequential planning	Integrated planning
Network Design & Management	Local planning tools	Dynamic planning tools	Integral planning tools
	Local performance indicators	Local performance indicators	Joint performance indicators
Transparency	Agreements about confidentiality and accessibility of data	Procedures/ scenarios informa- tion exchange (timeliness)	Joint development of information flows and databases
Connectivity	Web site status EDI-messages	Standard messages –EDI Datahub	Integration/ interfacing of planning systems

Table 4: Development paths

Even without explicitly including opportunities for mutually coordinated planning in the chain, practice has shown that transparency and connectivity are in themselves significant steps. It is only at a later stage that more complex forms such as reciprocal co-ordination or dynamic planning are considered. In the business cases, this strategy was followed by Tulip co and Food co. Both organisations judged that the step towards connectivity and transparency would already comprise a major challenge. Including closer co-ordination and planning would be too complex.

Step 4: Overall design and choice of IT logistics service provider
The final step of the ILC Scan is, in fact, the first step towards the implementation of the Intelligent Logistics Concept: the actual elaboration of the ILC design. The design comprises two steps: a detailed functional design and a system design. The detailed functional design involves specifying the new method of managing the logistic chain and allocating roles and tasks. The system design involves the design information and communication systems for supporting the management of the chain. On the basis of the system design, a Request for Information (RFI) and a Request for Quotation (RFQ) can be submitted to several ICT service providers, after which a detailed design for an information and communication system can be worked out with the selected provider or providers.

7   Epilogue

The analysis of the business cases and the examples presented elsewhere in this book show that ILC can contribute to the improvement of supply chain performances in many different ways. Because of a lack of general concepts and process descriptions of collaborative planning (as developed for CPFR), the organizations participating in the business cases have developed ILCs themselves, tailored to their own supply chain situation. By describing the business cases, identifying some generic elements and lessons from the business cases in this last chapter, we have attempted to present some useful examples and elements of ILC that allow organizations to identify the opportunities and benefits of ILC in their own supply chain.

The examples and the forms and characteristics of ILC are a first step towards an ILC Scan. An ultimate ILC Scan ought to present a refined classification of forms of ILC and a more detailed and practical approach to the identification of opportunities and the selection of the most appropriate form of inter-organizational co-ordination. To allow organizations to apply the ILC Scan by themselves, both the forms of collaboration and the steps of the ILC Scan need further work. The step-by-step approach needs to be extended with a questionnaire and a tool to evaluate the answers (like the tool developed by Involvation and the CPFR Roadmap). In the Supply Chain Collaboration in the Chemical Industry[2] project, a theoretical and conceptual

---

[2] see Appendix A for brief description of the project

158

CHAPTER 8

model of supply chain collaboration, a questionnaire and evaluation tool will be developed to fill this gap.

8   Acknowledgements

The authors would like to thank Justus Becker, Babiche van de Loo and Annelies van der Ham for their contributions to earlier versions of this chapter.

9   References

Bensao, N (1997), "Portfolio of buyer-supplier relationships", Sloan Management Review, summer, pp. 35-43

Edwards, P./Peters, M./Sharman, G. (2001), "The effectiveness of information systems in supporting the extended supply chain", Journal of Business Logistics, Vol 22, No 1, pp. 1-27.

Goor, A.R. van/Ploos van Amstel, M.J./Ploos van Amstel, W. (1999), *Fysieke Distributie: denken in toegevoegde waarde*, Educatieve Partners Nederland, Houten (4e druk).

Involvation (2002), Quick Test - CPFR en VMI; Test effect en haalbaarheid voor uw organisatie (Quick test – CPFR and VMU: test the impact and feasibility to your organization), www.involvation.com.

Kumar, K./Dissel, H.G. van (1996), "Sustainable Collaboration: Managing Conflict and Co-operation in Inter-Organizational Systems", MIS Quarterly, 20(3).

McCann, J. E./Galbraith, J. R. (1981), "Interdepartmental relations", in: Nystrom, P.C./ Starbuck, W.H. (Eds.), *Handbook of organizational design*, Oxford University Press, New York.

Oosteren, H. van (2002), "E-logistics oplossingen: kostenbesparing en kwaliteitsver-betering voor logistieke processen", Tijdschrift voor Inkoop en Logistiek, Jan/Feb, pp.22-25.

Thompson, J. D. (1967). *Organizations in action*, McGraw-Hill, New York.

Ven, A. H. van de/Delbecq, A. L./Koenig Jr, R. (1976), "Determinants of Coordination Modes Within Organizations", American Sociological Review, 41 (April), pp. 322-338.

VICS (1999), *Roadmap to CPRF: the case studies*, available at www.cpfr.org

VICS (2000), *CPFR Guidelines*, available at www.cpfr.org

Appendix A: ILC projects supported by Connekt

In the period 2001-2003, Connekt has supported various projects in which aspects of Intelligent Logistics Concepts were analysed, developed and implemented. This appendix contains a brief summary of each of these projects.

Intelligent Logistics Concepts: articulating demand

In the project 'ILC-Demand' the needs for and opportunities of Intelligent Logistics Concepts are examined in specific logistic chains. The objective is to formulate requirements and wishes for the further development of Intelligent Logistics Concepts and to chart the experiences of shippers and transporters with ICT, planning and collaboration. Through three workshops discussions haven taken place with shippers and service providers on three topics: 1) How are businesses already implementing ILC, 2) How to achieve improvements in transparency and connectivity in the chain 3) What is the need for the development and exchange of knowledge in this area. The selected industries were: spare parts and electronics.

Intelligent Logistics Concepts: IT-systems

The objective of the 'IT systems' project is to stimulate the development of new tools and to achieve greater compatibility in the development of Intelligent Logistics Concepts among IT-solutions. In a series of workshops IT-providers are brought together to discuss the needs and conditions for a more coordinated approach to the development of new tools. Starting point of the discussions are some specific applications that need to be developed or are in an early stage of development. By means of these cases the needs and benefits of a coordinated approach are discussed to avoid the wheel being invented more than once and to guarantee compatibility between different types of solutions of provided by different IT providers.

Netherlands Logistics Datahub

The objective of the project "Netherlands Logistics Datahub" is to show how the competitive position of logistics service providers and shippers could be strengthened by improving their supply chain capabilities. The enabler for this improvement is the development and introduction of a logistics datahub. The logistics datahub ensures that providers of logistics services have faster access to information and a number of ICT functions, which give transparency to the whole logistic chain. The core of the concept is that each of the players (only) communicates with the datahub, instead of many bilateral communication relations, and the datahub passes the information to all the parties that require this information for planning and control of the logistic process. In the project, the current situation is analysed for seven logistic chains and the added value of a datahub is charted

Flora Flower Auctions Logistics Datahub

Flora Flower Auctions is one of the largest cooperative flower auctions in the world. The auction in Naaldwijk receives large quantities of flowers and plants from growers every day. These flowers and plants need to be delivered to various merchants and are sorted by Flora via a cross-dock operation. Up to now, Flora receives hardly any logistics information from the growers, transporters and merchants as to the types and quantities that will be delivered to them and at what time. The transporters do not know in advance precisely what quantities they will be collecting from the grower and at what time they can deliver to Flora. As a result, there are waiting times for the docks and the internal process of Flora is reactive. The Logistics Datahub for Floriculture is an IT platform in which the information from the relevant parties is linked. The growers, Flora and the transporters will thus be enabled to make the supply trajectory transparent and to optimise it to their advantage.

Vos Logistics Datahub Pilot

The container chain Veendam–Rotterdam is characterised by a large number of chain parties (truck operators, rail service centre, barge operator, stevedore, shipping company, etc.) Vos Logistics coordinates the chain operations and decides when and with which modality a container is transported between Rotterdam and Veendam. The most important logistic requirement for these parties in the chain is the moment of availability of the container. In other words, when can the next party in the chain have access to the container? Currently, information exchange between the various transport chain parties is far from optimal. This causes delays in the transport of containers and inefficient use of resources (no shows of containers). The Vos Logistics Datahub will connect all the parties in the chain by providing connectivity and a specially developed data structure. The datahub provides transparency to all transport chain parties on the actual and future status of containers and allows Vos Logistics to improve the planning and monitoring of the transport chain.

Vos Logistics Datahub: Experiences and knowledge

The objective of the project Vos Logistics Datahub: experiences and knowledge is to make the 'experience and knowledge components' resulting from the Vos pilot widely available. This will consist partially of a description of the implementation course of the datahub and the analysis of the implementation process. The following questions will be answered:

- What is the IT situation for each of the parties (which systems, etc.)?
- What information/reports are being exchanged?
- Which technical adaptations are required?
- Which organisational adaptations are required?
- What are the expected advantages per party if all the communication takes place via the datahub?
- What are the implementation costs, etc.?

Logistics Datahub Workshops: Flora Flower Auctions and Vos Logistics

The improvement of logistic chains is generally not a Greenfield approach in which a new intelligent logistics concept is introduced but it builds upon existing market structures and logistic processes. As this usually concerns a complex network of independent, but strongly related organisations. These existing relationships and coordination mechanisms already in place form the departure point for improvements. Intelligent Logistics Concepts are thus constructed bottom-up. Examples of strongly related sectors with a large number of independent companies are floriculture and container logistics. The concept of the logistics datahub is being discussed with parties within the sector in two workshops on the basis of the Flora Holland and Vos Logistics pilots. The discussions in the workshops are aimed at the advantages, pre-conditions and success factors for a sector-wide introduction and use of the datahub.

Flora Flower Auctions Logistics Datahub: Experiences and knowledge

In 2001 Flora Flower Auctions participated in the development of the Logistics Datahub pilot. In the pilot a logistics datahub for Floriculture was implemented. The hub facilitates the logistic information exchange between growers, transporters and the flower auctioneers is. In this project the pilot is evaluated and the experiences are assessed.

- How was the datahub at Flora Flower Auctions set up, which alternatives were considered/choices made (both technological and organisational)?
- Which implementation process was followed with the datahub and how will this subsequently be evaluated?
- Which advantages/disadvantages have there been for the individual chain parties as a result of the pilot datahub and which are potentially feasible?
- Which follow-up steps are required to develop the datahub further?

Advanced Logistics Information Exchange

In this exploratory study, a new method of connectivity between logistic enterprises is being examined with the aim of increasing the transparency in logistic chains. The purpose of the project is to show the potential of a distributed environment of logistic data exchange. The feasibility and applicability is demonstrated on the basis of a simple prototype. The application assists transport organisations to exchange loads and capacity in a single step instead of approaching their colleagues and electronic markets individually. At the same time the project will facilitate further development of this principle. On the basis of these insights, an application in intelligent agent environment can be developed. The acceptance factors and the effects of the use of a distributed environment will be evaluated by a user group. In this way the user requirements of logistic service providers are incorporated explicitly.

Binnenlloyd Business Case and Pilot

Binnenlloyd Maastricht and Cementbouw wish to expand its services to shippers, receivers and other parties involved in the transport of bulk loads (fly ash, lime, cement). For instance, Cementbouw and Binnenlloyd can combine Vendor Managed Inventory with ship scheduling by triggering replenishment of inventory in case ships become idle. The central question is whether it is possible to improve the information exchange and connectivity between all the parties in the chain through the use of state-of-the-art information and communication technology (ICT) to such an extent that the processes become transparent for all parties and permit intelligent, collaborative planning with advantages for all the parties in the chain. The objective of the pilot is to test the possibilities for following ships and to capture data from the ship, the load and the position with Binnenlloyd. Binnenlloyd expects to obtain a better insight into the status of ships as a result. Binnenlloyd also expects that the reporting between Binnenlloyd and the ships will become more consistent and of a higher quality. Ultimately the service provision to clients must be improved. This is a unique project for the inland waterways, as a large part of the chain will be involved.

Distrivaart 2 (Distribution waterways 2)

The central objective of the Distrivaart 2 is 'to development and implement a multimodal, national, intelligent transhipment network that combines road transport and inland waterways for combined transport freight flows on pallets between manufacturing locations, transfer locations and retailers' distribution centres'. The project focuses on the requirements from different perspectives: economics, network design, warehouse and transhipment technology, and planning and control. The Planning and Control study defines the decisions that need to be made in the planning and monitoring of the processes of the various actors in the network and how they need to be coordinated. The result of the analysis is a blue print of the planning and control principle, a system design and a market review on the availability of software needed to implement the planning and control system. Some gaps in the availability have been identified as subjects for further development.

THEMIS Supply and Demand

THEMIS is the Network of industry and research professionals that focuses on the role of Freight Transport within the European Intelligent Transport Systems (ITS). The aim of the network is to understand and communicate how information - both from traffic management and from freight transport management - can best be made available for improving the quality of freight transport management and vice versa. The THEMIS thematic network is funded by the European Commission DG TREN - Directorate General for Transport and Energy. The objective of the 'Supply and Demand' project is to focus on the Dutch situation by using the insights of using traffic information in freight transport management developed within the EU and to disseminate the results and lessons from other countries in the Netherlands.

Exploring the application of Intelligent Agents in Logistic Chains

Central to this project is an exploration of the practical applicability of Intelligent Agents in the logistics sector. A number of logistics and chain applications are selected (purchasing, resource sharing, planning) to identify how Agent Technology can improvement supply chain coordination by increasing the information processing capabilities and the speed of interaction on linkages in the supply chain. To this end, knowledge about the potentials of Intelligent Agents are shared with from different players in the logistic chain (creation of awareness) and discussions take place to determine in which processes in the logistic chain Agent Technology can be applied and what added value (qualitative) this technology will bring.

Approach

Barge transportation plays an important role in hinterland transportation from and to Rotterdam taking approximately a 40% market share all containers routed through Rotterdam. A major challenge is the planning of the barge container loading an unloading process. On average, a barge visits up to eight terminal during a round trip in the port. Furthermore, delays occur frequently and the planning is disturbed. Barge operators do not have sufficient information on the availability of capacity at the terminals to compose an efficient round trip or to reschedule their round trip. So far, solutions suggesting a centralized planning or information system have been rejected by the industry. In this project, the opportunities offered by agent technology are analyzed to investigate how coordination in the port can be improved without losing decentralized decision making by barge operators and terminal operators.

Intelligent Logistics Concepts: Knowledge and Strategy

The objective of the project 'ILC-Knowledge and Strategy' is the generalisation and dissemination of the results from the programme and the positioning of this knowledge within the development and initiatives that are taking place worldwide. To this end the terminology of supply chain management and collaborative planning is first briefly explained, an overview of the results of ILC projects is given and a framework for the development of knowledge in the field of ILC and a method for the evaluation of pilots is proposed.

Supply Chain Collaboration in the Chemical Industry

In high tech and automotive industries much progress is made in establishing advanced supply chain collaboration and collaborative planning. In the chemical industry collaboration is just emerging. The objective of this project is to identify the drivers and appropriate concepts for supply chain collaboration in the chemical industry. In three selected supply chains (two of DSM and one of Solvay) the potential benefits of supply chain collaboration will be identified. Together with the supply chain partners in these three supply chains, a design for supply chain collaboration is developed. The experiences from the selected supply chains are the basis for the generalisation of results to chemical industry in general.

Appendix B: ILC projects supported by KLICT

Shortened Fresh Collection

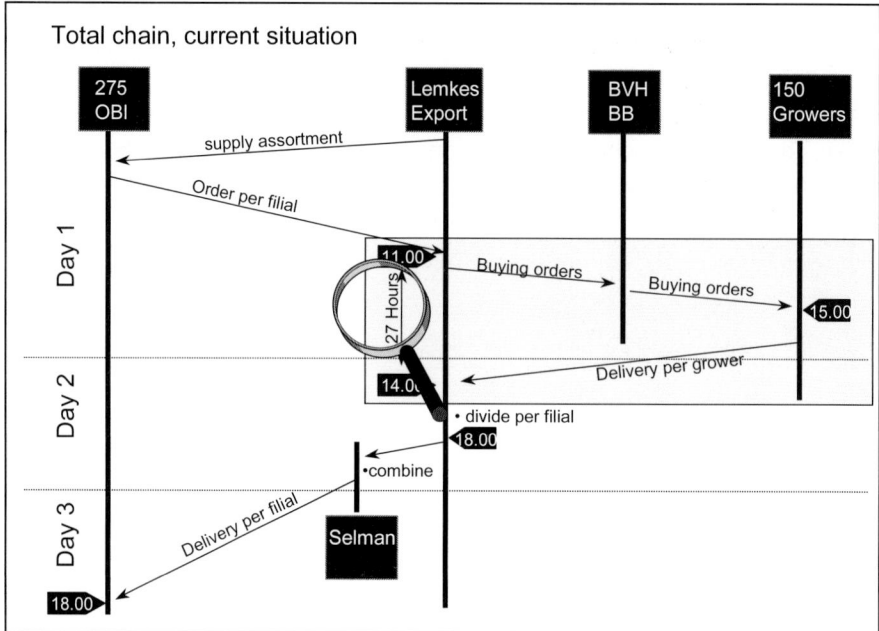

Total chain, current situation

Objective	To clarify and significantly reduce the lead time of the product range for a chain, from the moment the exporter places an order to the time of actual delivery to the exporter's premises. This should be followed by scaling up by means of developing a universally applicable solution with which to reduce the lead times of an ornamental plant cultivation cluster.
Output	Tool: Agro Logistics model at chain and cluster level
	Tool: ICT Toolkit for measuring the performance at chain and cluster level
	Tool: Detailed implementation handbook for cluster-wide application of the Agro Logistics model for lead time reduction
	Business case
	Final report
Sectors/ participants	Sector: Ornamental plant cultivation
	Knowledge consumers: Flora flower auction, Lemkes and SLN
	Knowledge suppliers: ATO
Social importance	The project is aimed at optimising the logistics processes of the ornamental plant cultivation network in Bleiswijk. This will lay the foundation for reducing social problems regarding accessibility, sustainability and lack of space.

Via Collect

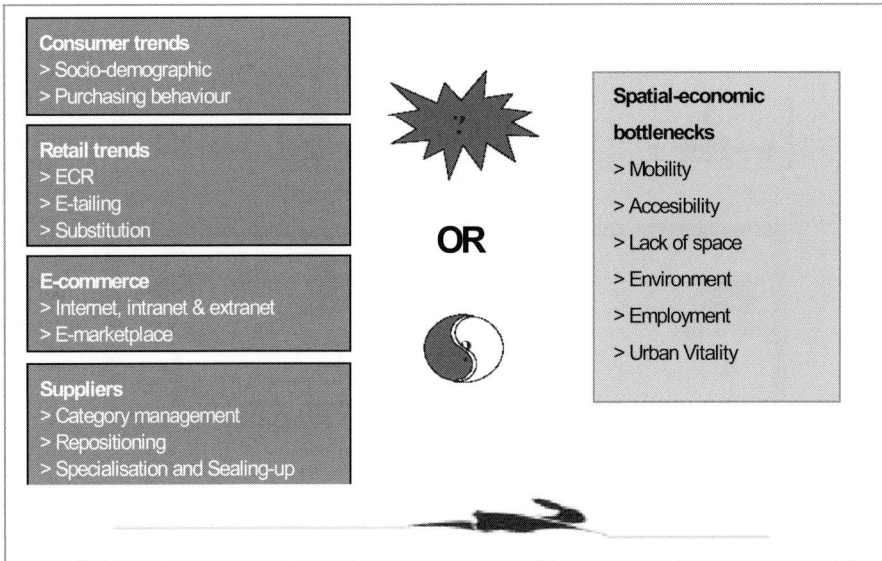

Objective   To develop an ICT and marketing model for a take-away chain (logistics fulfilment) in response to the logistic needs of both business users and consumers. The marketing model involves the identification of 'early adapters'. The ICT model concerns the development of an information architecture.

Output   'Contours of a generic information architecture' Report
Tool: Static object model, representing relevant roles, objects and services and the types of interrelationships
Tool: Dynamic model, representing object life cycles and actions geared to those projects
Marketing report
Workshop, held 4 March 2002: Project-based contribution to launch of Via Collect
Workshop, held 18 April 2002: Project-based contribution to KLICT/HIDC 'Electronic payment methods in logistics fulfilment' workshop
Final report

Sectors/participants   Sector: Logistics services and retail
Knowledge consumers: Via Collect, Schadebo, FGN, De Kruidenier, HIDC and Ericsson
Knowledge suppliers: TNO-FEL E-Business and Tilburg University

Social importance   The project contributes to a logistics concept, according to which the unused transport capacity of home or office-bound consumers can be utilised to carry packages, such as shopping and components, to their final destination. This would substantially reduce transport mileage and environmentally harmful emissions and improve the accessibility of urban areas.

Chase 'Chain service'

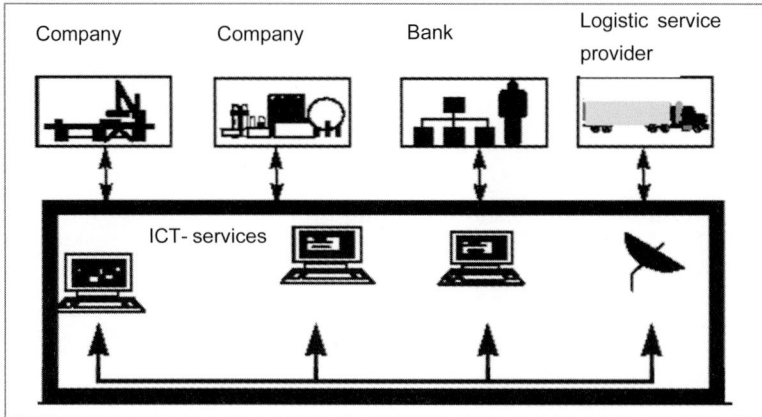

Objective	The principal aim is to lay a generic, flexible and chain-wide (inter-enterprise) ICT foundation for chain co-ordination and collaboration. In addition, the project defines solutions for two fundamental problems in chain-wide ICT, viz. structural and semantic heterogeneity between parties. This is an innovative project, as it is based on generality, flexibility and a chain-wide approach.
Output	State-of-the-art overview of developments in the area of harmonisation activities for information systems across chains. Most activities were found to be focused mainly on message structure, whereas it is necessary to work on standardisation at the semantic level.
	Number of tools (or elements) in order to facilitate heterogeneous information systems across chains (tools and solutions for semantic reconciliation), particularly interesting and usable for science and applied research institutes
	Scientific publication by TI
	Awareness that standardisation and organisation of Platforms (e.g. for payment transactions (credit card) and the telecommunications industry) is also necessary for tracking and tracing-like systems in order to meet social requirements regarding transparency
Sectors/ participants	Knowledge consumers: Descartes Systems Group, Flora flower auction and TNT
	Knowledge suppliers: Telematica Instituut
Social importance	A better awareness of the progress of flows within chains facilitates chain manageability and optimal utilisation of resources. The project thus contributes to a well-considered utilisation of resources, reduction of mileage, etc.

Fruitful

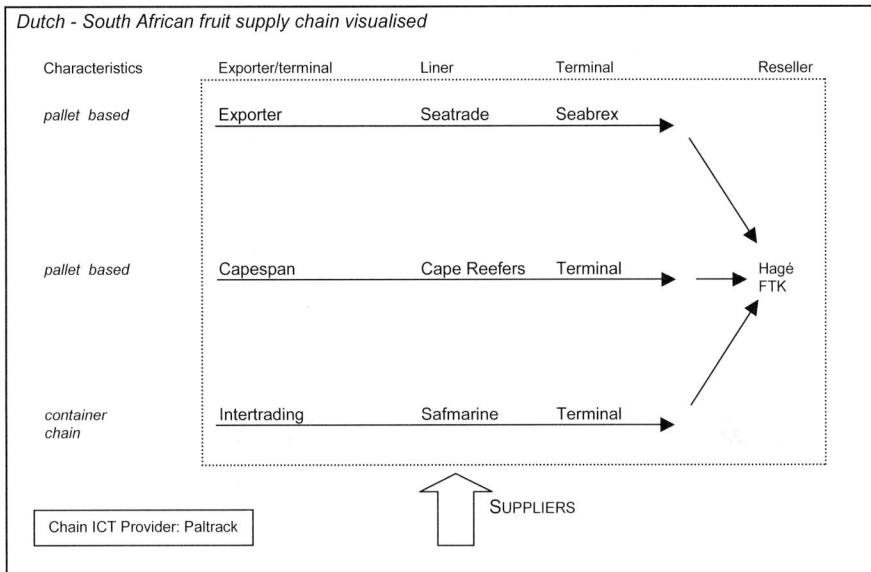

Dutch - South African fruit supply chain visualised

Characteristics	Exporter/terminal	Liner	Terminal	Reseller
pallet based	Exporter	Seatrade	Seabrex	
pallet based	Capespan	Cape Reefers	Terminal	Hagé FTK
container chain	Intertrading	Safmarine	Terminal	

SUPPLIERS

Chain ICT Provider: Paltrack

Objective	To assess the potential benefits and investment costs of an integrated supply chain information system, which eliminate the disadvantages of the current situation. The current 'island' systems all focus on one part of the supply chain and do not dovetail with one another. Moreover, there are no uniform standards and the quality aspects are somewhat neglected.
Output	Detailed analysis of logistic performance in the three pilot fruit chains
	Detailed analysis of product quality in the chain at specific times
	Generic model of an integral logistics and quality information system
	Scientific paper
	Business case
	Final report
Sectors/ participants	Sector: Fruit trade and distribution sector
	Knowledge consumers: Hagé international, Seabrex, Seatrade, Intertrading, Capespan, Paltrack, Rotterdam Port Management, FTK, Safmarine, PPECB, Ministry of Agriculture, Nature Management and Fisheries, SANTF
	Knowledge suppliers: TNO Inro, ATO and CSIR transportek (South Africa)
Social importance	The project helps enhance the quality of products, as it enables chain parties to trace where products are and assess the quality of products at particular times in the chain. In addition, it helps improve opportunities for the primary sector, the distribution sector and the fruit trade sector.

Collaborative Replenishment

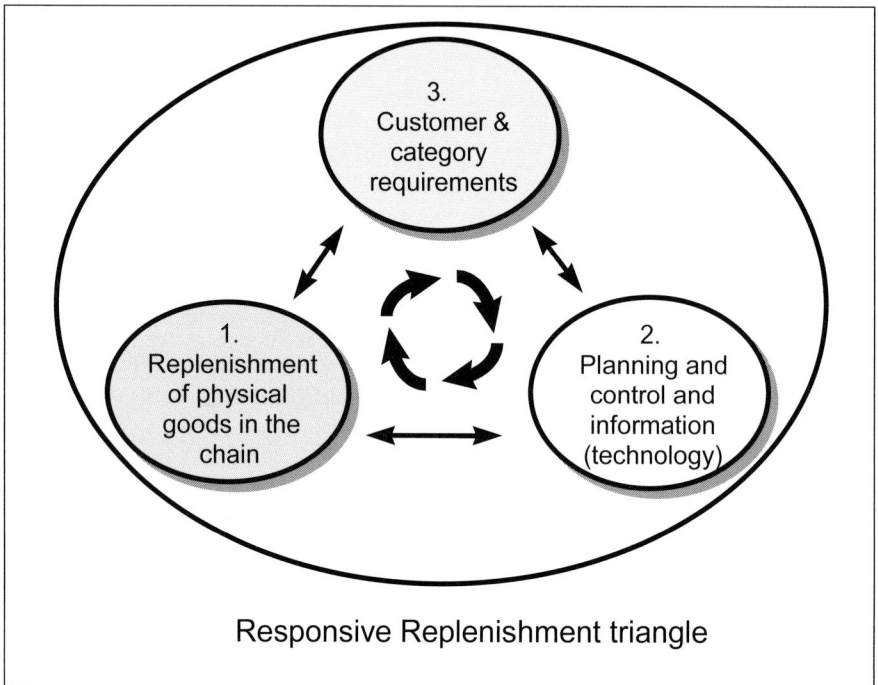

Responsive Replenishment triangle

Objective	To increase the chain responsiveness between a retailer and an exporter of potted plants by translating customer requirements into demands to be placed on the supply chain.
Output	Position paper: Benchmark case for modelling alternative supply chains Tool: Replenishment model Final report
Sectors/ participants	Sector: Ornamental plant cultivation Knowledge suppliers: LEI, Tilburg University, Wye College (UK) and Rijnconsult Knowledge consumers: Lemkes (exporter), B&Q (retailer), FloraHolland and Greensystems
Social importance	The project provides solutions to the existing pressure on the environment and the accessibility of the transport network. Every supplier has its own method of optimising its logistics. Integration of all optimisation methods makes it possible to find new ways of making better use of the loading capacity of lorries and reducing mileage, especially when return flows can be combined.

Appendix C: Addresses

ICES Foundations

KLICT

Rompertsebaan 70, P.O Box 3060, 5203 DB 's- Hertogenbosch,
The Netherlands
T: +31 (0)73-5286650
www.klict.org

Contact persons:

Ms. B.P.A.M. van de Loo
Project manager Reconfiguration
E: vandeloo@klict.org

Mr. K. Geijzers
Project manager Reconfiguration
E: geijzers@klict.org

Ms. M. Freriks
Project manager Knowledge management and Communication
E: freriks@klict.org

Connekt

Kluyverweg 6, P.O. Box 48, 2600 AA Delft, The Netherlands
T: +31 (0)15 – 251 65 65,
www.connekt.nl

Contact persons:

Ms. M. Leijnse,
Programme manager Freight &Mobility
E: leijnse@connekt.nl

Ms. J. Lops
Public Relations and Communication
E: lops@connekt.nl

Authors

H. Akkermans

Eindhoven University of Technology. Technology Management,
P.O. Box 513, 5600 MB Eindhoven, The Netherlands.
T: +31 (0)40-2474977/2230
F: +31 (0)40-2464596
E: h.a.akkermans@tm.tue.nl

and

Minase B.V.,
Fabriekstraat 1a, 5038 EM Tilburg The Netherlands
P.O. Box 278, 5000 AG Tilburg, The Netherlands.
T: +31 (0)13-5443468
F: +31 (0)13-5446864
E: henk@minase.nl

P. Bogerd

Minase B.V.,
Fabriekstraat 1a, 5038 EM Tilburg, The Netherlands
P.O. Box 278, 5000 AG Tilburg, The Netherlands.
T: +31 (0)13-5443468
F: +31 (0)13-5446864
E: paul@minase.nl

J. van Doremalen

CQM B.V.,
Vonderweg 11, P.O. Box 414, 5600 AK Eindhoven, The Netherlands.
T: +31 (0)40-2755771
F: +31 (0)40-2758712
E: vdm@cqm.nl

B. van Eck

Illyan B.V.
Sarphatistraat 642, 1018 AV Amsterdam, The Netherlands
T: +31 (0)20-5209550
F: +31 (0)20-5209551
E: Bvaneck@illyan.nl

G.W. Guis

TNO Inro
Schoemakerstraat 97, P.O. Box 6041, 2600 JA Delft, The Netherlands
T: +31 (0)15-2696831
F: +31 (0)15-2696854
E: g.w.guis@inro.tno.nl

J. van Hillegersberg

Erasmus University Rotterdam, Faculty of Business Administration
P.O. Box 1738, 3000 DR Rotterdam, The Netherlands
T: +31 (0)10-4082624
F: +31 (0) 10-4089010
E: j.hillegersberg@fbk.eur.nl

M. Kentrop

Illyan B.V.
Sarphatistraat 642, 1018 AV Amsterdam, The Netherlands
T: +31 (0)20-5209550
F: +31 (0)20-5209551
E: MKentrop@illyan.nl

M. Leenaarts

Illyan B.V.
Sarphatistraat 642, 1018 AV Amsterdam, The Netherlands
T: +31 (0)20-5209550
F: +31 (0)20-5209551
E: Mleenaarts@illyan.nl

B.P.A.M van de Loo

Erasmus University Rotterdam, Faculty of Business Administration
P.O. Box 1738, 3000 DR Rotterdam, The Netherlands
T: +31 (0)10-4081175
F: +31 (0)10-4089014
E: bloo@fbk.eur.nl

and

KLICT
Rompertsebaan 70, P.O Box 3060, 5203 DB 's- Hertogenbosch,
The Netherlands
T: +31 (0)73-5286650
E: vandeloo@klict.org

M. Melis

Initi8
Torenwacht 98, 2353 DC Leiderdorp, The Netherlands
T: +31 (0)71-5899830
F: +31 (0)71-5899816
M: +31 (0)6-45436736
E: melis@initi8.nl

I. Miller

Initi8
Torenwacht 98, 2353 DC Leiderdorp, The Netherlands
T: +31 (0)71-5899830
F: +31 (0)71-5899816
M: +31 (0)6-45436736
E: miller@initi8.nl

J.A.E.E. van Nunen

Erasmus University Rotterdam, Faculty of Business Administration
P.O. Box 1738, 3000 DR Rotterdam, The Netherlands
T: +31 (0)10-4082201
F: +31 (0)10-4089010
E: j.nunen@fbk.eur.nl

M. van Oosterhout

Erasmus University Rotterdam, Faculty of Business Administration
P.O. Box 1738, 3000 DR Rotterdam, The Netherlands
T: +31 (0)10-4088816
F: +31 (0)10-4089010
E: m.oosterhout@fbk.eur.nl

W. Ploos van Amstel

TNO Inro
Schoemakerstraat 97, P.O. Box 6041, 2600 JA Delft, The Netherlands
T: +31 (0)15-2696876
F: +31 (0)15-2696854
E: w.ploosvanamstel@inro.tno.nl

M. Rustenburg

TNO Inro
Schoemakerstraat 97, P.O. Box 6041, 2600 JA Delft, The Netherlands
T: +31 (0)15-2696828
F: +31 (0)15-2696854
E: m.rustenberg@inro.tno.nl

F.-P. Scheer

ATO b.v.
Bornsesteeg 59
6700 AA Wageningen
T: +31 (0)317-478552
F: +31 (0)317-475347
E: frans-peter.scheer@wur.nl

M.C. Schut

Vrije Universiteit Amsterdam, Department of artificial intelligence,
Faculty of Science, De Boelelaan 1081a, 1081 HV Amsterdam,
The Netherlands
T: +31 (0)20-444 7668
F: +31 (0)20-444 7653
E: schut@cs.vu.nl

J. Treur

Vrije Universiteit Amsterdam, Department of artificial intelligence,
Faculty of Science, De Boelelaan 1081a, 1081 HV Amsterdam,
The Netherlands,
T: +31 (0)20-444 7763
F: +31 (0)20-444 7653
E: treur@cs.vu.nl

and

Universiteit Utrecht, Faculty of philosophy
Heidelberglaan 8, 3584 CS Utrecht, The Netherlands
T: +31 (0)30-253 2698
F: +31 (0)30-253 2816
E: treur@cs.vu.nl

J.C.M. Tseng

Erasmus University Rotterdam, Faculty of Business Administration
P.O. Box 1738, 3000 DR Rotterdam, The Netherlands
T: +31 (0)10-4082854
F: +31 (0)10-4089010
E: j.tseng@fbk.eur.nl

T.M. Verduijn

TNO Inro
Schoemakerstraat 97, P.O. Box 6041, 2600 JA Delft, The Netherlands
T: +31 (0)15-2696861
F: +31 (0)15-2696854
E: tmv@inro.tno.nl

P. de Wit

HIDC, P.O Box 660, 2700 AR Zoetermeer, The Netherlands
T: +31 (0)79-3438125
F: +31 (0)79-3479217
E: p.dewit@ndl.nl

R.A. Zuidwijk

Erasmus University Rotterdam, Faculty of Business Administration
P.O. Box 1738, 3000 DR Rotterdam, The Netherlands
T: +31 (0)10-4082235
F: +31 (0)10-4089010
E: r.zuidwijk@fbk.eur.nl